Old Indian Days

OLD INDIAN DAYS

BY
CHARLES A. EASTMAN
(Ohiyesa)

Introduction by A. LaVonne Brown Ruoff

University of Nebraska Press
Lincoln and London

Introduction copyright © 1991 by the University of Nebraska Press
Manufactured in the United States of America

First Bison Book printing: 1991
Most recent printing indicated by the last digit below:
10   9   8   7   6   5   4   3   2

Library of Congress Cataloging-in-Publication Data
Eastman, Charles Alexander, 1858–1939.
Old Indian days / by C. A. Eastman (Ohiyesa): introduction by A.
LaVonne Brown Ruoff.
p. cm.
Reprint, with new introd. Originally published : New York: McClure
Co., 1907.
ISBN 0-8032-6718-5
1. Dakota Indians—Fiction.   2. Indians of North America—Fic-
tion.   I. Title.
PS3509.A74804   1991
813'.52—dc20
90-25561   CIP

Reprinted from the original 1907 edition published by the McClure
Company

To

My Daughters

DORA, IRENE, VIRGINIA, ELEANOR, AND FLORENCE

I Dedicate

these Stories of the Old Indian Life,

and especially of

the Courageous and Womanly Indian Woman

CONTENTS

INTRODUCTION
By A. LaVonne Brown Ruoff

One of the first collections of short fiction to be published by an Indian author, *Old Indian Days* (1907) vividly depicts the life and customs of Sioux bands in Minnesota and the Dakotas from the early eighteenth century through the 1860s. Although earlier Indian authors incorporated ethnohistory and oral literature and reinterpretations of traditional stories into their autobiographies, Charles A. Eastman (Ohiyesa) and his collaborator, Elaine Goodale Eastman, blended these elements with contemporary fiction. In doing so they established a precedent followed by later Indian writers of short fiction.[1]

From the early twentieth century through the 1930s, Charles Eastman was probably the best-known writer and lecturer on American Indian life and issues. Charles's parents were descended from generations of Santee leaders of the Wahpeton and Mdewakanton bands. His father was Ite Wakanhdi Ota (Many Lightnings), a Wahpeton whose father and grandfathers had been chiefs. Many Lightnings' mother, Uncheedah, was a granddaughter of Mahpiya Wichasta (Cloud Man), a Mdewakanton chief who was one of the earliest Santee converts to Christianity. Charles's mother was Wahkantankanwin (Goddess), whose grandfather was Seth Eastman, a white New Englander, and whose grandmother was at least one-fourth French. Wahkantankanwin's English name was Mary Nancy Eastman. Charles was born in 1858 near Redwood Falls, Minnesota. Shortly thereafter, Wahkantankanwin died, leaving motherless four sons and a daughter. Given the name of Hakadah (The Pitiful Last), Charles was raised primarily by his paternal grandmother, Uncheedah, who educated him as a traditional Santee Sioux boy, far from contact with whites. Separated from his father and two brothers after

the 1862 Sioux Uprising, Charles fled with his relatives and other
Santees to Canada. His life as a traditional Santee ended at age fifteen when he was reunited with his father. Imprisoned for three
years for his role in the 1862 Minnesota Sioux uprising, Many
Lightnings converted to Christianity and took the name Jacob
Eastman. After his release he eventually settled in 1869 near
Flandreau, Dakota Territory, and then traveled to Canada to find
his son. Convinced that Indians must adapt to white ways, Jacob
persuaded his son to return to Flandreau with him and enroll in
school. During the next seventeen years, Charles attended Beloit
College, Dartmouth College (class of 1887), and Boston Univer-
sity Medical School. When he graduated from the latter in 1890,
Eastman was one of the first American Indian doctors. Just before the Ghost Dance religion swept through the Sioux nation,
Charles became an agency physician at Pine Ridge, in what is now
South Dakota. In the fall of 1890, he and Elaine Goodale (1863–
1953) met and became engaged a month later. Both helped to
care for those caught in or fleeing from the fighting at Wounded
Knee, which began on December 29.

Descended from staunch New England stock, Elaine was primarily educated at Sky Farm, her home in the Berkshires of western Massachusetts. As children, both Elaine and her sister Dora
published in journals poetry that received considerable praise.
The appearance of their collected poems in *Apple Blossoms: Verses
of Two Children* (1878), which sold over ten thousand copies,
brought them acclaim in the United States and England. When
Elaine's family lacked the money to send her to college, she became in 1883 a teacher in the American Indian Department of
Hampton Institute, Virginia. She also became an effective public
relations writer for the Institute. Resolved to devote her life to being an Indian educator, Elaine toured the Great Sioux Reservation in 1884. The following year she opened a school on the west
bank of the Missouri at the mouth of the White River. In 1890 she
was appointed as the first supervisor of Indian education in the
two Dakotas.

Married in New York City on June 18, 1891, the Eastmans returned to Pine Ridge after their honeymoon. By early 1883,

Charles's disputes with authorities over policy became so intense that he resigned his position and moved his growing family to St. Paul. There he tried unsuccessfully to establish a medical practice.

Charles later served as an outing agent for Carlisle Indian School and as physician for the Crow Creek Sioux Agency from 1900 to 1903, a position he also left as a result of another dispute with the agent. During the next two decades, Charles held a number of positions in Indian affairs: Indian secretary for the International YMCA, legal representative for the lower Santee Indians in their land claims against the government, and clerk to revise the Sioux allotment rolls. He was also active in organizations like the American Indian Association (later called the Society of American Indians). In 1915 the Eastmans purchased a New Hampshire summer camp, which was a major source of income until 1921.

The Eastman family eventually included six children: Dora, Virginia, Irene, Eleanor, Florence, and Ohiyesa II (Charles Alexander). Over the years, however, the couple grew apart. Undoubtedly, continuing financial problems, different backgrounds and world views, and Charles's frequent absences as he pursued various projects must have created tensions that exacerbated after the death of their daughter, Irene, in 1918. Three years later the Eastmans separated. Charles spent most of the winter months of the next eighteen years in the Detroit area near his son, Ohiyesa II. In 1939, after a tepee in which he had been living caught fire, Charles suffered smoke inhalation and then contracted both pneumonia and a heart condition, which killed him on January 8. Elaine died in 1953.

The couple collaborated on the books issued under Charles's name. In *From the Deep Woods to Civilization*, Charles acknowledged Elaine's contributions to his books: "The present is the eighth that I have done, always with the devoted cooperation of my wife. Although but one book, *Wigwam Evenings*, bears both our names, we have worked together."[2] On April 19, 1939, Elaine described the collaboration in greater detail to Harold G. Rugg: "Dr. Eastman's books left his hand . . . as a rough draft in pencil, on scratch paper." From these she typed copies, "revising, omitting, and rewriting as necessary."[3] The first book published under Eastman's name was the inaugural volume of Charles's autobiography, *Indian Boyhood* (1902). Written for his children, this book chronicles Charles's life from childhood to age fifteen and depicts traditional Sioux life. The popularity of *Indian Boyhood* inspired the Eastmans to write three collections that included reinterpretations of legends and their own fiction. *Red Hunters and the Animal People* (1904) combines myths with adventure and animal stories based on common experiences and observations of Indian hunters. *Old Indian Days* (1907) was followed by *Wigwam Evenings: Sioux Folktales Retold* (1909).

Charles also published several works of nonfiction. *Soul of the Indian* (1911) is a discussion of Indian religion based on a Sioux model. *The Indian To-day* (1915) surveys Indian history, Native Americans' contribution to the United States, their achievements, reservation life, and current problems. In 1916 Charles published the second volume of his autobiography, *From the Deep Woods to Civilization*, describing his experiences in the white world. Here he reveals a deepening sense of his own Indianness and questions the superiority of white ways. Among his most interesting works is *Indian Heroes and Great Chieftains* (1918), which either the leaders themselves or their contemporaries told Eastman. Although he remained an active spokesman on Indian affairs and continued to write, he published no books after his separation from Elaine.

In addition to collaborating with her husband, Elaine was a vigorous writer on Indian issues as well as a novelist, poet, biographer, and playwright. Her earliest works of fiction are *Little Brother o' Dreams* (1910) and *Yellow Star: A Story of East and West* (1911), which she termed "potboilers." She also interpreted tribal myths in *Indian Legends Retold* (1919. Her more mature novels are *The Luck of Old Acres* (1928) and *One Hundred Maples* (1935), her best work of fiction. Her collected poetry was published in *The Voice at Eve* (1930). In addition, she wrote a biography, *Pratt, The Red Man's Moses* (1935). *Sister to the Sioux* (1978), written in the 1930s and published posthumously, is a memoir of her life among the Sioux from 1885 to 1891. She also wrote a number of un-published plays on Indian themes.[4]

II

Since the nineteenth century, the Sioux have typified the nobility and ferocity of the Plains Indian to most Americans and have served as the prototype for Indians in western novels and, later, movies. In the mid-seventeenth century, when the tribe was first mentioned by French explorers, they were Woodland Indians, divided into seven bands or "council fires," many of which appear in *Old Indian Days*. Located just west of the Great Lakes, they inhabited the southern two-thirds of what is now Minnesota as well as adjacent parts of Iowa, Wisconsin, and the Dakotas. Pressure from the Ojibwas, their hereditary enemies who had been armed by the French, and the depletion of game caused them to move westward and to split into three great divisions: the eastern, or Santee; the middle, or Dakota; and the western, or Teton.

The fascinating history of the Sioux from contact through the end of the nineteenth century has often been told. Here a word about the Minnesota Sioux Uprising of 1862 is in order because it had personal consequences for Charles Eastman and because it forms the background for three of the stories in *Old Indian Days*. After the War of 1812, during which the Sioux sided with the British as they had during the Revolutionary War, the United States government initiated a series of treaties designed to move the Sioux westward and then onto reservations. Under pressure from white settlement, the eastern Dakotas or Santees signed the Treaty of 1837, the Treaty of Traverse des Sioux, and the Treaty of Mendota (the latter two signed in 1851), relinquishing all claims to land in Minnesota. In exchange they accepted settlement on reservations along the Minnesota River above New Ulm in southwestern Minnesota near the South Dakota boundary and extending to Stone Lake, 140 miles north. In 1858 they gave up the ten-mile strip north of the Minnesota River. One of the chief negotiators of this treaty was Little Crow (ca. 1818–1863). The Eastmans charge in "The Chief Soldier" that Little Crow was induced by the traders to sign over the purchase price of part of the Santee reservation (p. 118). By 1862 Dakotas were incensed about delayed payment of annuities and were feuding with traders over whether the annuities for the 1858 settlement paid all Indians' debts or only those incurred prior to the agreement. Congress exacerbated the situation by failing to pass the legislation necessary to feed and house the Dakotas. Tribal members also resented white settlement on what they viewed as their hunting grounds. Tensions erupted on August 17, when four or six Indians, primarily from Rice Creek village, killed Robinson Jones, who had apparently sold whiskey to the Indians, and five other whites. The Indians then reported their action to the members of the soldier's lodge at Rice Creek. After a consensus for war was reached, a group of warriors marched to Little Crow's house. Although the Eastmans characterize Little Crow as seizing "his opportunity to show once and for all to the disaffected that he had not love for the white man" (p. 118), Gary Clayton Anderson concludes in *Little Crow* that few men were dragged more reluctantly into war. The next day, Little Crow and his forces launched the attack on the Lower Santee Agency described in "The Chief Soldier" (pp. 114–33).[5] Little Crow became one of the the primary leaders of the Sioux Uprising. The conflict ended on September 23, when Colonel Henry H. Sibley's troops defeated the chief's warriors in the Battle of Wood Lake.

The Uprising had severe consequences for the Santee. Nearly four hundred full- and mixed-bloods were tried by a military tribunal and 303 (including Eastman's father, Many Lightnings) were sentenced to be hanged. President Abraham Lincoln reprieved all but 39 Santees, 38 of whom were hanged en masse in Mankato. Others, like Many Lightnings, were imprisoned. Enraged whites successfully pressured the government to remove the Santees from Minnesota, some of whom returned over the years. Some of the Santees, including Eastman's relatives, fled to Canada during the conflict. In May 1863 Little Crow tried unsuccessfully to gain permission of the authorities to settle his hungry, suffering people in Canada. Returning to Minnesota, Little Crow was killed in July while gathering berries. By November 1863, the

Sioux began to straggle into Fort Garry (now Winnipeg) Mani-
toba, where they were reduced to begging for food.
Over three thousand Sioux had arrived in the Red River Métis
settlement by spring 1864. In "The Famine" (pp. 100–113), the
Eastmans portray the near-starvation endured in Canada by a
band of exiles led by White Lodge, described as Little Crow's son.
The group is saved by Angus McLeod, whose father was a trader.[6]
The 1862 Uprising also affected relationships between groups of
Sioux. "The White Man's Errand" (pp. 134–48) describes how a
young Zuyamani is pursued in the winter of 1863 by Sioux hostile
to his band, the Hunkpatees (Lower Yanktonai or Hunkpatina of
the Dakota division). This group remained loyal to the United
States during the Uprising.

III

Divided into stories about "The Warrior" and "The Woman," *Old
Indian Days* primarily focuses on individuals whose actions illustrate Sioux history, customs, and values. Three stories portray the
interrelationship between the Sioux and animals: "The Grave of
the Dog,"[7] "Snana's Fawn," and "The Faithfulness of Long Ears."
The tales, which were published in such popular magazines of the
day as *Harper's Bazaar* and *Metropolitan,* are set in a period that
ranges from the turn of the eighteenth century through the
1860s. The stories in "The Warrior" section depict the code of be-
havior, rituals, and challenges experienced by warriors from ado-
lescence onward. The fullest and most complex portrayal of these
is "The Love of Antelope," which provides detailed information
about Sioux warrior rituals, courtship, and mourning customs.
Although the story depicts the fearless courage expected of a
Sioux warrior, it also portrays the deep love such a warrior can
feel, in this case for Taluta, who dies, and for her "twin spirit,"
Stasu, who is an enemy Arikara. Out of love for Stasu, Antelope
forsakes his tribe.
    In "The Chief Soldier," the Eastmans dramatize the dilemma
faced by Tawasuota (Many Hails), a Wahpeton Santee warrior
torn between duty to Chief Little Crow and the safety of his band

and family. This story, based on actual characters and events, describes the consequences of Tawasuota's decision to obey the unjust command from Chief Little Crow that he fire the first shot in the band's attack on the Lower Santee Agency. Because he has accepted the position as Little Crow's chief soldier, Tawasuota reluctantly kills James W. Clark, a clerk in the store owned by traders Nathan and Andrew J. Myrick.[8] The consequences of this act are immediate: a chief who is a relative chastises Tawasuota for precipitating the loss of the country and destruction of their nation, his mother is distraught over his action, and his wife leaves with his children to seek safety among the whites. A loving father, Tawasuota risks his life to see his sons one last time. He later dies in battle.

The danger of unreasoning adherence to the warrior code of honor, pride, and loyalty is vividly illustrated in "The Madness of Bald Eagle." Friendly relations between the Sioux and the Arikaras, their longtime enemies, end abruptly when a Yanktonai warrior kills Bald Eagle, an Arikara, on a dare. The result is a bloody battle between the Arikaras and the Mandans on one side and the Yanktonais and Blackfoot Sioux on the other. The story accurately depicts the fierce and unremitting warfare that the Sioux waged against the Arikaras and Mandans in the mid-nineteenth century.[9]

Although the other stories in "The Warrior" section deal exclusively with full-bloods, "The Singing Spirit" also includes a Canadian Métis, Antoine Michaud, as a central character. The exciting description of Michaud's death-defying attack on a buffalo herd pays tribute to the first generation of Canadian Métis, whom the Eastmans call "the greatest hunters of the bison" (p. 88).

The focus on "The Woman" in the second and longest section of *Old Indian Days* is particularly significant because few contemporary ethnographies of American Indians and autobiographies dealt with women.[10] "Winona, Woman-Child" and "Winona, Child-Woman" give a particularly detailed account of women's lives from birth through marriage and analyze the role they played in Sioux society. "Winona, Child-Woman" contains the Eastmans' fullest statements about the place of the Sioux woman:

"She is the foundation of man's dignity and honor. Upon her rest the life of the home and of the family" (p. 184).

"Blue Sky," "The War Maiden," and "The Peace-Maker" illustrate the courage of Sioux women. In "Blue Sky," the heroine sneaks into the enemy Crow camp to find her lover, whom she discovers has been adopted by the tribe in recognition of his bravery. "The War Maiden[11] recounts the exploits of Makatah, who loved war since childhood and, armed only with a coupstick, leads a Sioux attack against the Crows. According to the Eastmans, it was not unusual in the old days for a woman to go to war. "The Peace-Maker," one of the best character portraits in the book, illustrates the bravery of Eyatónkawa (She Whose Voice I Heard Afar). In hand-to-hand combat, this fearless Wapakute woman killed a Sac who tried to murder her. Reciting the story of her triumph, Eyatónkawa stops the armed, half-drunk Chief Tamáhay[12] from killing another warrior. No less brave in her later years, Eyatónkawa saves her band from some drunken warriors who plot to kill Little Crow[13] by reminding them that they should kill enemies, not each other.

The role of woman as mediator is the theme of "She Has a Soul," which takes place on Lake Superior at the turn of the eighteenth century. When a Catholic priest is captured, the chief's daughter persuades her father not to kill him.[14] The same theme runs through the story of Dowanhotaninwin, told in "Winona, Woman-Child." Dowanhotaninwin goes off with a Sac and Fox warrior whose tribe killed her parents. Her act brings about peace between the tribes.[15]

In *Old Indian Days* the Eastmans primarily emphasize plot and ethnography, although they also include some stories that focus on character, such as "The Chief Soldier," "The War Maiden," and "The Peace-Maker." The sometimes melodramatic plots, generally noble characters, and romantic style of their stories reflect both the literary tradition of earlier depictions of American Indians and popular taste of the times. These elements are present as well in the works of such nineteenth and early twentieth-century Native American authors as George Copway (Ojibwa), John Rollin Ridge (Cherokee), Alexander Posey (Creek), and

Emily Pauline Johnson (Mohawk). The descriptions of characters sometimes border on stereotype. Antelope is called a "princely youth" who possesses a "stoic visage" ("The Love of Antelope," pp. 3, 19). Anookasan is described in "The Singing Spirit" as being "of the original native type" (pp. 77) while Magaskawee in "The Famine" is characterized as "piquant" and as "one of the belles of the forest" (p. 101). Occasionally, the style lapses into purple prose, which may reflect Elaine's poetic inclinations. In "Winona, the Woman-Child," the heroine is portrayed as "the robust beauty of the wild lily of the prairie, pure and strong in her deep colors of yellow and scarlet against the savage plain and horizon, basking in the open sun like a child, yet soft and womanlike, with drooping head when observed" (p. 182).

The romanticism of some of the language and characterizations is counterbalanced by the more direct style the Eastmans use to create exciting scenes of pursuit and combat. It is also counterbalanced by their careful delineation of Sioux rituals, customs, and camp life; use of oral history; and incorporation of Sioux phrases. Their recreation of Sioux storytelling in some of the narratives adds further authenticity. For example, Chief White Ghost of the Yanktonais relates "The Madness of Bald Eagle." In "The White Man's Errand," Zuyamani recounts his adventures as he carried the white soldier's message to Fort Berthold, while in "The War Maiden," Smokey Day,[16] a respected tribal historian and famed storyteller, narrates Makatah's story. In "Winona, Woman-Child," the author breaks into the narrative to tell the story about Dowanhotaninwain. The Eastmans enrich their book by emphasizing the importance of the oral history and literature. In "Winona, the Woman-Child," two grandmothers tell the baby girl legends of "their most noted female ancestors, from the twin sisters of the old story, the maidens of the star people of the sky,[17] down to their own mothers" (p. 174). "The Famine" contains an allusion to mythic Eyah or Iyah, whom the Eastmans describe as the god of famine. In "The Singing Spirit," the discussion of myths about Chanotedah or Oglugechana become an important part of the plot. This story was published previously in *Sunset Magazine*.[18]

INTRODUCTION xix

Long out of print, *Old Indian Days* offers readers a fascinating glimpse into Sioux life prior to the twentieth century. Like the Eastmans' many other books on Indians, it is an enjoyable and important contribution to our knowledge of this nation's Native Americans.

NOTES

1. Other Sioux who reinterpreted their tribe's oral literature, narrated autobiographies, or wrote accounts of their lives or tribe in the first half of the twentieth century include Ella C. Deloria, Black Elk, Marie McLaughlin, Standing Bear, and Zitkala-Ša.

2. Charles Eastman, *From the Deep Woods to Civilization*, pp. 185–86.

3. Quoted in Raymond Wilson, *Ohiyesa: Charles Eastman, Santee Sioux*, p. 130.

4. Biographical information about Charles A. and Elaine Goodale Eastman has been derived from Ruth Ann Alexander, "Elaine Goodale Eastman and the Failure of the Feminist Protestant Ethnic"; David R. Miller, "Charles Alexander Eastman, The 'Winner'"; and Wilson, *Ohiyesa*.

5. Taoyateduta (His Red Nation), who became Little Crow V, was a Mdewakanton Santee descended from four generations of tribal leaders called Little Crow. After leaving two Wakpekute Santee wives in 1838, he eventually married four daughters of Inyangami, leader of a Sisseton band of the Wahpeton. Eastman wrote a short biography of Little Crow in *Indian Heroes and Chieftains* (1907). In *Little Crow*, Gary Anderson stresses that the chief had little choice but to sign the 1858 treaty. Little Crow angrily protested against it and against the government's failure to fulfill the terms of the 1851 treaty until Indian Commissioner Charles Mix made it clear that if the delegation did not sign the document, the government would take the Sioux land without compensation. The treaty did produce some money to pay trade debts (pp. 95–104).

Anderson also emphasizes that Little Crow initially refused the Rice Creek warrior's demand that he join them in war against the whites. As the young men taunted and threatened him, Little Crow relented, declaring, "You will die like the rabbits when the hungry wolves hunt them in the Hard Moon [January]. Ta-o-ya-te-du-ta is not a coward: he will die with you" (p. 132).

6. The Canadian government eventually established reserves for var-

ious groups of Sioux. The present Birdtail Reserve was established near Fort Ellice (called "Ellis" by the Eastmans in "The Famine") at the junction of Birdtail Creek with the Assiniboine River. See Anderson, *Little Crow* (pp. 171–76); Roy W. Meyer, *The History of the Santee Sioux,* Chapter 6; and James H. Howard, *The Canadian Sioux,* pp. 25–32.

Although the Eastmans identify White Lodge as a son of Little Crow, this name does not appear among Little Crow's sons, whose names Anderson lists in his genealogies (p. 193). The names of Little Crow's children by his Wakpekute wives are not known.

The allusion in the story to the Scotch trader McLeod (p. 100) may refer to Martin McLeod or his family. McLeod ran a post at Lac qui Parle in Santee territory during the nineteenth century. See Anderson, *Little Crow,* pp. 43, 52, 54, 59.

7. "The Grave of the Dog" originally appeared in *Metropolitan Magazine* 23 (February 1906); 569.

8. At 7:00 a.m. on August 18, Little Crow's men attacked the Lower Santee Agency. Tawasuota shot Clark as he stood in the doorway of the store owned by Myrick. See Anderson, *Little Crow* (pp. 135–36). According to Esther Wakeman (known as Mahpiyatowin or Blue Sky Woman), daughter of Wakianheida or Going Higher, two men from the agency told her that they had been eating breakfast "when Ta-wa-su-ota suddenly appeared in the room and shot the storekeeper. My brother who had been sitting next to the storekeeper became covered with blood and fainted." When she arrived, the store had been ransacked: "I turned my head and saw a white man hiding. He said, 'Don't speak to me.' Ta-wa-su-ota appeared in the doorway and shot at him. He escaped through a window." (*Through Dakota Eyes,* ed. Gary Clayton Anderson and Alan R. Woolworth, pp. 54–55). For a discussion of Eastman's treatment of history in *Old Indian Days* and other works, see Anna Lee Stensland, "Charles Alexander Eastman."

9. The agricultural tribes of Arikara, Mandan, and Hidatsa were easy prey for the Sioux, who raided them constantly between 1845 and 1862. The Treaty of Fort Laramie (1851), assigning territory to these tribes, did not halt Sioux raids, which increased in intensity in 1861. Although they would have preferred to live separately, the three tribes sought safety together near Fort Berthold in North Dakota. See Roy W. Meyer, *The Village Indians of the Upper Missouri* (pp. 101–10), and Joseph H. Cash and Gerald W. Wolf, *The Three Affiliated Tribes* (pp. 45–48).

10. In the first half of the twentieth century, two Sioux women wrote books about women in their tribe: *American Indian Stories* (1921) by Zitkala-Ša contains stories about the author's and other women's lives and

Waterlily (1988) by Ella C. Deloria chronicles the life of the title character from childhood to adulthood. Completed in the 1940s, the novel was published posthumously.

11. "The War Maiden" was originally published in the *Ladies Home Journal* 23 (August 1906): 14.

12. Tamáhay, Tamaha, or Tanazin (d. 1860), also known as L'Original Levé or Standing Moose, was one of only two of his nation to serve on the American side in the War of 1812. He was subchief of the Red Wing Mdewakanton. Eastman included a short biography of him in *Indian Heroes and Great Chieftains*. See also Roy W. Meyer, *History of the Santee Sioux*, pp. 25–26, 33.

13. The plot of Little Crow's half-brothers to kill him occurred in 1845, when Little Crow appeared at his father's village to claim the chieftainship. Warned by his half-brothers that if he landed he would die, Little Crow challenged them to "shoot then, where all can see." A ball from a rifle knocked Little Crow down, breaking the bones of his forearms. The wound caused Little Crow's wrists to be deformed for the rest of his life. See Eastman, "Little Crow," *Indian Heroes and Great Chieftains*, and Anderson, *Little Crow*, p. 44. In their biographies of Little Crow, neither Eastman nor Anderson record the story told in "The Peace-Maker."

14. Published accounts of encounters between priests and the Sioux, which date back to 1640, do not refer to the incident depicted in this story. In *A New Discovery of a Vast Country in America* (1697), Louis Hennepin describes his experiences as a Sioux captive in 1680.

15. The story of Dowahotaninwin, which deals with the Sioux's conflicts with the Sac and Fox, probably occurs in the early nineteenth century. The main goal of the Treaty of Prairie du Chien (1830) was to stop raids by the two groups on one another. Although the treaty created a neutral strip between Sioux and Sac and Fox territory, raiding continued for another decade. See Meyer, *History of the Santee Sioux*, pp. 50–51.

16. Smokey Day appears as the storyteller in *Indian Boyhood* and *Wigwam Evenings*. A Mdewankanton named "Smokey Day" was one of the sons of Cloud Man, Eastman's paternal great grandfather. This Smokey Day was a close companion of Little Crow during the 1840s. See Anderson, *Little Crow*, p. 190.

17. A reference to the Star-Husband myth, widespread on the Great Plains. In this myth, two sisters fall in love with Star husbands, whom they accompany to the sky. Once there, they long to return to earth.

18. "The Singing Spirit" was published in *Sunset Magazine* 20 (1907): 112–21.

AUTHORS AND WORKS CITED

Alexander, Ruth Ann. "Elaine Goodale Eastman and the Failure of the Feminist Protestant Ethic." *Great Plains Quarterly* 8 (1988): 89–101.

Anderson, Gary Clayton. *Kinsmen of Another Kind: Dakota-White Relations in the Upper Mississippi Valley, 1650–1862.* Lincoln: University of Nebraska Press, 1984.

———. *Little Crow: Spokesman for the Sioux.* St. Paul, Minnesota Historical Society Press, 1986.

Anderson, Gary Clayton and Alan R. Woolworth, eds. *Through Dakota Eyes: Narrative Accounts of the Minnesota Indian War of 1862.* St. Paul: Minnesota Historical Society Press, 1988.

Black Elk. John Neihardt. *Black Elk Speaks. Being the Life Story of a Holy Man of the Oglala Sioux.* 1932. Reprint. Introduction by Vine Deloria, Jr. Lincoln: University of Nebraska Press, 1979.

Carley, Kenneth. *The Sioux Uprising of 1862.* St. Paul: Minnesota Historical Society, 1976.

Cash, Joseph H. and Gerald W. Wolff. *The Three Affiliated Tribes (Mandan, Arikara, and Hidatsa).* Phoenix: Indian Tribal Series, 1974.

Deloria, Ella C., ed. *Dakota Texts.* Publications of the American Ethnology Society 17 (1932). Reprint. New York: AMS, 1974. Reprint. Agnes Picotte and Paul N. Pavich, eds. Vermillion: University of South Dakota Press, 1978. English version only.

———. *Speaking of Indians.* 1944. Reprint. Agnes Picotte and Paul N. Pavich, eds. Vermillion: University of South Dakota Press, 1979.

Eastman, Charles A. *From the Deep Woods to Civilization: Chapters in the Autobiography of an Indian.* 1916. Reprint. Introduction by Raymond Wilson. Lincoln: University of Nebraska Press, 1977.

———. *Indian Boyhood.* 1902. Reprint. New York: Dover, 1971.

———. *Indian Heroes and Great Chieftains.* Boston: Little, Brown, 1918.

———. *The Indian To-day: The Past and Future of the First Americans.* 1915. Reprint. New York: AMS, 1975.

———. *The Soul of the Indian: An Interpretation.* 1911. Reprint. Lincoln: University of Nebraska Press, 1980.

———. *Red Hunters and the Animal People.* 1904. Reprint. New York: AMS, 1976.

——— and Elaine Goodale Eastman. *Wigwam Evenings: Sioux Tales Retold.* 1909. Reprint. Introduction by Michael Dorris and Louise Erdrich. Lincoln: University of Nebraska, 1990.

Eastman, Elaine Goodale and Dora Reed Goodale. *Apple Blossoms: Verses of Two Children.* New York: Putnam's, 1878.

————. *Good Sister to the Sioux: The Memories of Elaine Goodale Eastman, 1885–91.* Ed. Kay Graber. Lincoln: University of Nebraska Press, 1978.

————. *Little Brother o' Dreams* Boston: Houghton Mifflin, 1910.

————. *One Hundred Maples.* Brattleboro, Vt.: Stephen Day Press, 1935.

————. *Pratt, The Red Man's Moses.* Norman: University of Oklahoma Press, 1935.

————. *The Voice at Eve.* Chicago: Bookfellows, 1930.

————. *Yellow Star: A Story of East and West.* Boston: Little, Brown, 1911.

Hennepin, Louis. *Nouvelle Decouverte d'un tres grand Pays Situé dans l' Amerique.* (1697). Translated as *A New Discovery of a Vast Country in America.* 2nd ed. 1698. Reprint. Reuben Gold Thwaites, ed. 1903. Reprint. New York: Kraus Reprint Company, 1972.

Howard, James H. *The Canadian Sioux.* Studies in the Anthropology of North American Indians Series. Lincoln: University of Nebraska Press, 1984.

————. *The Dakota or Sioux Indians: A Study in Human Ecology.* South Dakota Museum Anthropological Papers No. 2. Vermillion: Dakota Museum, South Dakota University, 1966.

McLaughlin, Marie. *Myths and Legends of the Sioux.* 1916. Reprint. Lincoln: University of Nebraska Press, 1990.

Meyer, Roy W. *History of the Santee Sioux: United States Indian Policy on Trial.* Lincoln: University of Nebraska Press, 1967.

————. *The Village Indians of the Upper Missouri: The Mandans, Hidatsas, and Arikaras.* Lincoln: University of Nebraska Press, 1977.

Miller, David R. "Charles Alexander Eastman, The 'Winner': From Deep Woods to Civilization." *American Indian Intellectuals.* Ed. Margot Liberty. 1976 Proceedings of the American Ethnological Society. St. Paul: West, 1978. 61–73.

Standing Bear, Luther. *Land of the Spotted Eagle.* 1933. Reprint. Foreword by Richard N. Ellis. Lincoln: University of Nebraska Press, 1978.

————. *My Indian Boyhood.* 1931. Reprint. Lincoln: University of Nebraska Press, 1988.

————. *Stories of the Sioux.* 1934. Reprint. Lincoln: University of Nebraska Press, 1988.

Stensland, Anna Lee. "Charles Alexander Eastman: Sioux Storyteller and Historian." *American Indian Quarterly* 3 (1977): 199–208.

Wilson, Raymond. *Ohiyesa: Charles Eastman, Santee Sioux.* Urbana: University of Illinois Press, 1983.

Zitkala-Ša [Gertrude Bonnin]. *American Indian Legends, Retold by Zitkala-*

Ša. 1901. Reprint. Introduction by Agnes Picotte. Lincoln: University of Nebraska Press, 1985.

————. *American Indian Stories.* 1921. Reprint. Introduction by Dexter Fisher. Lincoln: University of Nebraska Press, 1985.

PART ONE
THE WARRIOR

I

THE LOVE OF ANTELOPE

I

UPON a hanging precipice atop of the Eagle Scout Butte there appeared a motionless and solitary figure—almost eagle-like he perched! The people in the camp below saw him, but none looked at him long. They turned their heads quickly away with a nervous tingling, for the height above the plains was great. Almost spirit-like among the upper clouds the young warrior sat immovable.

It was Antelope. He was fasting and seeking a sign from the " Great Mystery," for such was the first step of the young and ambitious Sioux who wished to be a noted warrior among his people.

He is a princely youth, among the wild Sioux, who hunts for his tribe and not for himself! His voice is soft and low at the campfire of his nation, but terror-giving in the field of battle. Such was Antelope's reputation. The more he sought the "Great Mystery" in solitude, the more gentle and retiring he became, and in the same proportion his courage and manliness grew. None could say that he was not a kind son and a good hunter, for he had already passed the "two-arrow-to-kill," his buffalo examination.

On a hot midsummer morning a few weeks later, while most of the inmates of the teepees were breakfasting in the open air, the powerful voice of the herald resounded among the pine-clad heights and green valleys.

"Hear ye, hear ye, warriors!" he chanted loudly. "The council has decreed that four brave young men must scout the country to the sunsetward of the camp, for the peace and protection of our people!"

All listened eagerly for the names of the chosen warriors, and in another moment there came the sonorous call: "Antelope, Antelope! the council has selected you!"

The camp was large—fully four hundred paces across; but in that country, in the clear morning air, such an announcement can be heard a great way, and in the silence that followed the hills repeated over and over the musical name of Antelope.

In due time the four chosen youths appeared before the council fire. The oath of the pipe was administered, and each took a few whiffs as reverently as a Churchman would partake of the sacrament. The chief of the council, who was old and of a striking appearance, gave the charge and command to the youthful braves.

There was a score or more of warriors ready mounted to escort them beyond the precincts of the camp, and the " fearless heart " song was sung according to the custom, as the four ran lightly from the door of the council teepee and disappeared in the woods.

It was a peculiarly trying and hazardous moment in which to perform the duties of a scout. The Sioux were encroaching upon the territory of hostile tribes, here in the foot-hills of the Big Horn Mountains, and now and then one of their hunters was cut off by the enemy.

[5]

If continual vigilance could not save them, it might soon become necessary to retreat to their own hunting-grounds.

It was a savage fetish that a warrior must be proof against the alluring ways of pretty maidens; that he must place his honor far above the temptations of self-indulgence and indolence. Cold, hunger, and personal hardship did not count with Antelope when there was required of him any special exertion for the common good. It was cause to him of secret satisfaction that the council-men had selected him for a dangerous service in preference to some of his rivals and comrades.

He had been running for two or three hours at a good, even gait, and had crossed more than one of the smaller creeks, yet many deep gulches and bad lands lay between him and the furthest peak that melted into the blue dome above.

" I shall stand upon the Bear's Heart," he said to himself. " If I can do that, and still report before the others, I shall do well! "

His keen eyes were constantly sweeping the

country in his front, and suddenly he paused and shrank back motionless in a crouching attitude, still steadily keeping an eye upon a moving object. It was soon evident that some one was stealthily eying him from behind cover, and he was outwitted by the enemy! Still stooping, he glided down a little ravine, and as he reached the bed of the creek there emerged from it a large gray wolf.

This was very opportune for Antelope. He gave the gray wolf's danger-call with all his might; waited an instant and gave it a second time; then he turned and ran fleetly down the stream. At the same moment the wolf appeared upon the top of the bank, in full view of the enemy.

" Here he comes! " they whispered, and had their arrows on the string as the wolf trotted leisurely along, exposing only his head, for this was a common disguise among the plains Indians. But when he came out into the open, behold! it was only a gray wolf!

" Ugh! " the Utes grunted, as they looked at each other in much chagrin.

" Surely he was a man, and coming directly into our trap! We sang and prayed to the gods of war when our war chief sent us ahead to scout the Sioux people, to find their camp. This is a mystery, a magic! Either he is a Sioux in disguise, or we don't know their tricks! " exclaimed the leader.

Now they gave the war-whoop, and their arrows flew through the air. The wolf gave a yelp of distress, staggered and fell dead. Instantly they ran to examine the body, and found it to be truly that of a wolf.

" Either this is a wonderful medicine-man, or we are shamefully fooled by a Sioux warrior," they muttered.

They lost several minutes before they caught sight of Antelope, who had followed the bed of the creek as far as it lay in his direction and then came out of it at full speed. It would be safer for him to remain in concealment until dark; but in the meantime the Ute warriors would reach the camp, and his people were unprepared! It was necessary to expose himself to the enemy. He knew that it would be chiefly a contest of speed and he had an excellent start; but on the other hand, the Utes doubtless had their horses.

"The Sioux who played this trick on us must die to-day!" exclaimed their leader. "Come, friends, we cannot afford to let him tell this joke on us at the camp-fires of his people!"

Antelope was headed directly for Eagle Scout Butte, for the camp was in plain view from the top of this hill. He had run pretty much all day, but then, that was nothing!

"I shall reach the summit first, unless the Ute horses have wings!" he said to himself.

Looking over his shoulder, he saw five horsemen approaching, so he examined his bow and arrows as he ran.

"All is well," he muttered. "One of their spirits at the least must guide mine to the spirit land!" where, it was believed by them, there was no fighting.

Now he was within hearing of their whoops, but he was already at the foot of the butte. Their horses could not run up the steep ascent, and they were obliged to dismount. Like a deer the Sioux leaped from rock to rock, and almost within arrow-shot came his pursuers, wildly whooping and yelling.

When he had achieved the summit, he took his stand between two great rocks, and flashed his tiny looking-glass for a distress signal into the distant camp of his people.

For a long time no reply came, and many arrows flew over his head, as the Utes approached gradually from rock to rock. He, too, sent down a swift arrow now and then, to show them that he was no child or woman in fight, but brave as a bear when it is brought to bay.

" Ho, ho! " he shouted to the enemy, in token of a brave man's welcome to danger and death.

They replied with yells of triumph, as they pressed more and more closely upon him. One of their number had been dispatched to notify the main war-party when they first saw Antelope, but he did not know this, and his courage was undiminished. From time to time he con-

tinued to flash his signal, and at last like lightning the little white flash came in reply.

The sun was low when the besieged warrior
discovered a large body of horsemen approaching from the northwest. It was the Ute war-
party! He looked earnestly once more
toward the Sioux camp, shading his eyes with
his right palm. There, too, were many moving
specks upon the plain, drawing toward the foot
of the hill!

At the middle of the afternoon they had
caught his distress signal, and the entire camp
was thrown into confusion, for but few of the
men had returned from the daily hunt. As
fast as they came in, the warriors hurried away
upon their best horses, singing and yelling.
When they reached the well-known butte, tow-
ering abruptly in the midst of the plain, they
could distinguish their enemies massed behind
the hanging rocks and scattered cedar-trees,
crawling up closer and closer, for the large war-
party reached the hill just as the scouts who
held Antelope at bay discovered the approach
of his kinsmen.

Antelope had long since exhausted his quiver of arrows and was gathering up many of those that fell about him to send them back among his pursuers. When their attention was withdrawn from him for an instant by the sudden onset of the Sioux, he sprang to his feet.

He raised both his hands heavenward in token of gratitude for his rescue, and his friends announced with loud shouts the daring of Antelope.

Both sides fought bravely, but the Utes at last retreated and were fiercely pursued. Antelope stood at his full height upon the huge rock that had sheltered him, and gave his yell of defiance and exultation. Below him the warriors took it up, and among the gathering shadows the rocks echoed praises of his name.

In the Sioux camp upon Lost Water there were dances and praise songs, but there was wailing and mourning, too, for many lay dead among the crags. The name of Antelope was indelibly recorded upon Eagle Scout Butte.

" If he wished for a war-bonnet of eagle feathers, it is his to wear," declared one of the young men. " But he is modest, and scarcely even joins in the scalp dances. It is said of him that he has never yet spoken to any young woman! "

" True, it is not announced publicly that he has addressed a maiden. Many parents would like to have their daughters the first one he would speak to, but I am told he desires to go upon one or two more war-paths before seeking woman's company," replied another.

" Hun, hun, hay! " exclaimed a third youth ill-naturedly. " He is already old enough to be a father! "

" This is told of him," rejoined the first speaker. " He wants to hold the record of being the young man who made the greatest number of *coups* before he spoke to a maiden. I know that there are not only mothers who would be glad to have him for a son-in-law, but their young daughters would not refuse to look upon the brave Antelope as a husband! "

It was true that in the dance his name was often mentioned, and at every repetition it seemed that the young women danced with more spirit, while even grandmothers joined in the whirl with a show of youthful abandon.

Wezee, the father of Antelope, was receiving congratulations throughout the afternoon. Many of the old men came to his lodge to smoke with him, and the host was more than gratified, for he was of a common family and had never before known what it is to bask in the sunshine of popularity and distinction. He spoke complacently as he crowded a handful of tobacco into the bowl of the long red pipe.

" Friends, our life here is short, and the life of a brave youth is apt to be shorter than most! We crave all the happiness that we can get, and it is right that we should do so. One who says that he does not care for reputation or success, is not likely to be telling the truth. So you will forgive me if I say too much about the honorable career of my son." This was the old man's philosophic apology.

"Ho, ho," his guests graciously responded. "It is your moon! Every moon has its fullness, when it lights up the night, while the little stars dance before it. So to every man there comes his full moon!"

Somewhat later in the day all the young people of the great camp were seen to be moving in one direction. All wore their best attire and finest ornaments, and even the parti-colored steeds were decorated to the satisfaction of their beauty-loving riders.

"Ugh, Taluta is making a maidens' feast! She, the prettiest of all the Unkpapa maidens!" exclaimed one of the young braves.

"She, the handsomest of all our young women!" repeated another.

Taluta was indeed a handsome maid in the height and bloom of womanhood, with all that wonderful freshness and magnetism which was developed and preserved by the life of the wilderness. She had already given five maidens' feasts, beginning with her fifteenth year, and her shy and diffident purity was held sacred by her people.

The maidens' circle was now complete. Behind it the outer circle of old women was equally picturesque and even more dignified. The

[15]

grandmother, not the mother, was regarded as the natural protector of the young maiden, and the dowagers derived much honor from their position, especially upon public occasions, taking to themselves no small amount of credit for the good reputations of their charges.

Weshawee, whose protégé had many suitors and was a decided coquette, fidgeted nervously and frequently adjusted her robe or fingered her necklace to ease her mind, for she dreaded lest, in spite of watchfulness, some mishap might have befallen her charge. Her anxiety was apparently shared by several other chaperons who stole occasional suspicious glances in the direction of certain of the young braves. It had been known to happen that a girl unworthy to join in the sacred feast was publicly disgraced.

A special police force was appointed to keep order on this occasion, each member of which was gorgeously painted and bedecked with eagle feathers, and carried in his hand a long switch with which to threaten the encroaching throng. Their horses wore head-skins of fierce

THE LOVE OF ANTELOPE

animals to add to their awe-inspiring appearance.

The wild youths formed the outer circle of the gathering, attired like the woods in autumn, their long locks glossy with oil and perfumed with scented grass and leaves. Many pulled their blankets over their heads as if to avoid recognition, and loitered shyly at a distance.

Among these last were Antelope and his cousin, Red Eagle. They stood in the angle formed by the bodies of their steeds, whose noses were together. The young hero was completely enveloped in his handsome robe with a rainbow of bead-work acros the middle, and his small moccasined feet projected from beneath the lower border. Red Eagle held up an eagle-wing fan, partially concealing his face, and both gazed intently toward the center of the maidens' circle.

"Woo! woo!" was the sonorous exclamation of the police, announcing the beginning of the ceremonies. In the midst of the ring of girls stood the traditional heart-shaped red stone, with its bristling hedge of arrows. In this case there were five arrows, indicating that Taluta had already made as many maidens' feasts. Each of the maidens must lay her hand upon the stone in token of her purity and chastity, touching also as many arrows as she herself has attended maidens' feasts.

Taluta advanced first to the center. As she stood for a moment beside the sacred stone, she appeared to the gazing bystanders the embodiment of grace and modesty. Her gown, adorned with long fringes at the seams, was beaded in blue and white across the shoulders and half way to her waist. Her shining black hair was arranged in two thick plaits which hung down upon her bosom. There was a native dignity in her gestures and in her utterance of the maidens' oath, and as she turned to face the circle, all the other virgins followed her.

When the feast was ended and the gay concourse had dispersed, Antelope and his cousin were among the last to withdraw. The young man's eyes had followed every movement of Taluta as long as she remained in sight, and it was only when she vanished in the gathering shadows that he was willing to retire.

In savage courtship, it was the custom to introduce one's self boldly to the young lady, although sometimes it was convenient to have a sister introduce her brother. But Antelope had no sister to perform this office for him, and if he had had one, he would not have made the request. He did not choose to admit any one to his secret, for he had no confidence in himself or in the outcome of the affair. If it had been anything like trailing the doe, or scouting the Ojibway, he would have ridiculed the very notion of missing the object sought. But this was a new warfare—an unknown hunting! Although he was very anxious to meet Taluta, whenever the idea occurred to him he trembled like a leaf in the wind, and profuse perspiration rolled down his stoic visage. It was not customary to hold any social intercourse with the members of the opposite sex, and he had never spoken familiarly to any woman since he became a man, except his old grandmother. It was well known that the counsel of the aged brings luck to the youth in warfare and love.

Antelope arose early the next morning, and without speaking to any one he made a ceremonious toilet. He put on his finest buckskin shirt and a handsome robe, threw a beaded quiver over his shoulder, and walked directly away from the teepees and into the forest—he did not know why nor whither. The sounds of the camp grew fainter and fainter, until at last he found himself alone.

"How is it," mused the young man, "that I have hoped to become a leader among my people? My father is not a chief, and none of my ancestors were distinguished in war. I know well that, if I desire to be great, I must deny myself the pleasure of woman's company until I have made my reputation. I must not boast nor exhibit myself on my first success. The spirits do not visit the common haunts of men! All these rules I have thus far kept, and I must not now yield to temptation. . . . Man has much to weaken his ambition after he is married. A young man may seek opportunities to prove his worth, but to a married man the opportunity must come to try him. He acts only when compelled to act. . . . Ah, I must flee from the woman! . . . Besides, if she should like someone else better, I should be humiliated. . . . I must go upon a long war-path. I shall forget her. . . ."

At this point his revery was interrupted by the joyous laughter of two young women. The melodious sing-song laughter of the Sioux maiden stirred the very soul of the young warrior.

All his philosophy deserted him, and he stood hesitating, looking about him as if for a chance of escape. A man who had never before felt the magnetic influence of woman in her simplicity and childlike purity, he became for the moment incapable of speech or action.

Meanwhile the two girls were wholly unconscious of any disturbing presence in the forest. They were telling each other the signals that each had received in the dance. Taluta's companion had stopped at the first raspberry bushes,

while she herself passed on to the next
thicket. When she emerged from the pines
into an opening, she suddenly beheld Antelope,
in his full-dress suit of courtship. Instantly
she dropped her eyes.

Luckily the customs of courtship among the
Sioux allow the covering of one's head with the
blanket. In this attitude, the young man made
a signal to Taluta with trembling fingers.

The wild red man's wooing was natural and
straightforward; there was no circumspection,
no maneuvering for time or advantage. Hot
words of love burst forth from the young
warrior's lips, with heavy breathing behind
the folds of the robe with which he sought to
shield his embarrassment.

" For once the spirits are guiding my fortunes! It may seem strange to you, when we
meet thus by accident, that I should speak immediately of my love for you; but we live in
a world where one must speak when the opportunity offers. I have thought much of you
since I saw you at the maidens' feast. . . . Is
Taluta willing to become the wife of Tatoka?

The moccasins of her making will cause his feet to be swift in pursuit of the game, and on the trail of the enemy. . . . I beg of you, maiden, let our meeting be known only to the birds of the air, while you consider my proposal!"

All this while the maiden stood demurely at his side, playing with the lariat of her pony in her brown, fine hands. Her doeskin gown with profuse fringes hung gracefully as the drooping long leaves of the willow, and her two heavy braids of black hair, mingled with strings of deers' hoofs and wampum, fell upon her bosom. There was a faint glow underneath her brown skin, and her black eyes were calm and soft, yet full of native fire.

"You will not press for an answer now," she gently replied, without looking at him. "I expected to see no one here, and your words have taken me by surprise. . . . I grant your last request. The birds alone can indulge in gossip about our meeting,—unless my cousin, who is in the next ravine, should see us together!" She sprang lightly upon the back of her pony, and disappeared among the scattered pines.

Between the first lovers' meeting and the second was a period of one moon. This was wholly the fault of Antelope, who had been a prey to indecision and painful thoughts. Half regretting his impulsive declaration, and hoping to forget his pangs in the chances of travel and war, he had finally enlisted in the number of those who were to go with the war-leader Crowhead into the Ute country. As was the custom of the Sioux warriors upon the eve of departure, the young men consulted their spiritual advisers, and were frequently in the purifying vapor-bath, and fasting in prayer.

The last evening had come, and Antelope was on the way to the top of the hill behind the camp for a night of prayer. Suddenly in the half-light he came full upon Taluta, leading her pony down the narrow trail. She had never looked more beautiful to the youth than at that moment.

" Ho," he greeted her. She simply smiled shyly.

"It is long since we met," he ventured.

"I have concluded that you do not care to hear my reply," retorted the girl.

"I have nothing to say in my defense, but I hope that you will be generous. I have suffered much. . . . You will understand why I stand far from you," he added gently. "I have been preparing myself to go upon the warpath. We start at daylight for the Ute country. Every day for ten days I have been in the vapor-bath, and ten nights fasting."

As Taluta well knew, a young warrior under these circumstances dared not approach a woman, not even his own wife.

"I still urge you to be my wife. Are you ready to give me your answer?" continued Antelope.

"My answer was sent to you by your grandmother this very day," she replied softly.

"Ah, tell me, tell me, . . ." pressed the youth eagerly.

"All is well. . . . Fear nothing," murmured the maiden.

"I have given my word—I have made my

prayers and undergone purification. I must not withdraw from this war-path," he said after a silence. " But I know that I shall be fortunate! . . . My grandmother will give you my love token. . . . Ah, kechuwa (dear love)! watch the big star every night! I will watch it, too—then we shall both be watching! Although far apart, our spirits will be together."

The moon had risen above the hill, and the cold light discovered the two who stood sadly apart, their hearts hot with longing. Reluctantly, yet without a backward look or farewell gesture, the warrior went on up the hill, and the maiden hurried homeward. Only a few moments before she had been happy in the anticipation of making her lover happy. The truth was she had been building air-castles in the likeness of a white teepee pitched upon a virgin prairie all alone, surrounded by mountains. Tatoka's war-horse and hunting pony were picketed near by, and there she saw herself preparing the simple meal for him! But now he has clouded her dreams by this untimely departure.

" He is too brave. . . . His life will be a

short one," she said to herself with foreboding.

For a few hours all was quiet, and just before the appearance of day the warriors' departure was made known by their farewell
songs. Antelope was in the line early, but he
was heavy of heart, for he knew that his sweetheart was sorely puzzled and disappointed by
his abrupt departure. His only consolation
was the knowledge that he had in his bundle
a pair of moccasins made by her hands. He
had not yet seen them, because it was the custom not to open any farewell gifts until the
first camp was made, and then they must be
opened before the eyes of all the young men!
It brings luck to the war-party, they said. He
would have preferred to keep his betrothal secret, but there was no escaping the custom.

All the camp-fires were burning and supper
had been eaten, when the herald approached
every group and announced the programme
for the evening. It fell to Antelope to open
his bundle first. Loud laughter pealed forth
when the reluctant youth brought forth a su-
perb pair of moccasins—the recognized love-

gift! At such times the warriors' jokes were unmerciful, for it was considered a last indulgence in jesting, perhaps for many moons. The recipient was well known to be a novice in love, and this token first disclosed the fact that he had at last succumbed to the allurements of woman. When he sang his love-song he was obliged to name the giver of the token, and many a disappointed suitor was astonished to hear Taluta's name.

It was a long journey to the Ute country, and when they reached it there was a stubbornly contested fight. Both sides claimed the victory, and both lost several men. Here again Antelope was signally favored by the gods of war. He counted many *coups* or blows, and exhibited his bravery again and again in the charges, but he received no wound.

On the return journey Taluta's beautiful face was constantly before him. He was so impatient to see her that he hurried on in advance of his party, when they were still several days' travel from the Sioux camp.

"This time I shall join in all the dances and

participate in the rejoicings, for she will surely like to have me do so," he thought to himself. "She will join also, and I know that none is a better dancer than Taluta!"

In fancy, Antelope was practicing the songs of victory as he rode alone over the vast wild country.

He had now passed Wild Horse Creek and the Black Hills lay to the southeast, while the Big Horn range loomed up to the north in gigantic proportions. He felt himself at home.

"I shall now be a man indeed. I shall have a wife!" he said aloud.

At last he reached the point from which he expected to view the distant camp. Alas, there was no camp there! Only a solitary teepee gleamed forth upon the green plain, which was almost surrounded by a quick turn of the River of Deep Woods. The teepee appeared very white. A peculiar tingling sensation passed through his frame, and the pony whinnied often as he was urged forward at a gallop.

When Antelope beheld the solitary teepee he knew instantly what it was. It was a grave!

Sometimes a new white lodge was pitched thus for the dead, who lay in state within upon a couch of finest skins, and surrounded by his choicest possessions.

Antelope's excitement increased as he neared the teepee, which was protected by a barricade of thick brush. It stood alone and silent in the midst of the deserted camp. He kicked the sides of his tired horse to make him go faster. At last he jumped from the saddle and ran toward the door. There he paused for a moment, and at the thought of desecrating a grave, a cold terror came over him.

"I must see—I must see!" he said aloud, and desperately he broke through the thorny fence and drew aside the oval swinging door.

II

In the stately white teepee, seen from afar, both grave and monument, there lay the fair body of Taluta! The bier was undisturbed, and the maiden looked beautiful as if sleeping, dressed in her robes of ceremony and surrounded by all her belongings.

Her lover looked upon her still face and cried aloud. "Hey, hey, hey! Alas! alas! If I had known of this while in the Ute country, you would not be lonely on the spirit path."

He withdrew, and laid the doorflap reverently back in its place. How long he stood without the threshold he could not tell. He stood with head bowed down upon his breast, tearless and motionless, utterly oblivious to everything save the bier of his beloved. His charger grazed about for a long time where he had left him, but at last he endeavored by a low whinny to attract his master's attention, and Antelope awoke from his trance of sorrow.

The sun was now hovering over the western ridges. The mourner's throat was parched, and perspiration rolled down his cheeks, yet he was conscious of nothing but a strong desire to look upon her calm, sweet face once more.

He kindled a small fire a little way off, and burned some cedar berries and sweet-smelling

grass. Then he fumigated himself thoroughly
to dispel the human atmosphere, so that the
spirit might not be offended by his approach,
for he greatly desired to obtain a sign from
her spirit. He had removed his garments and
stood up perfectly nude save for the breech-
clout. His long hair was unbraided and hung
upon his shoulders, veiling the upper half of
his splendid body. Thus standing, the lover
sang a dirge of his own making. The words
were something like this:

> Ah, spirit, thy flight is mysterious!
> While the clouds are stirred by our wailing,
> And our tears fall faster in sorrow—
>
> While the cold sweat of night benumbs us,
> Thou goest alone on thy journey,
> In the midst of the shining star people!
>
> Thou goest alone on thy journey—
> Thy memory shall be our portion;
> Until death we must watch for the spirit!

The eyes of Antelope were closed while he
chanted the dirge. He sang it over and over,
pausing between the lines, and straining as it
were every sense lest he might not catch the
rapt whisper of her spirit, but only the distant

howls of coyotes answered him. His body became cold and numb from sheer exhaustion, and at last his knees bent under him and he sank down upon the ground, still facing the teepee. Unconsciousness overtook him, and in his sleep or trance the voice came:

"Do not mourn for me, my friend! Come into my teepee, and eat of my food."

It seemed to Antelope that he faltered for a moment; then he entered the teepee. There was a cheerful fire burning in the center. A basin of broiled buffalo meat was placed opposite the couch of Taluta, on the other side of the fire. Its odor was delicious to him, yet he hesitated to eat of it.

"Fear not, kechuwa (my darling)! It will give you strength," said the voice.

The maid was natural as in life. Beautifully attired, she sat up on her bed, and her demeanor was cheerful and kind.

The young man ate of the food in silence and without looking at the spirit. "Ho, kechuwa!" he said to her when returning the dish, according to the custom of his people.

Silently the two sat for some minutes, while the youth gazed into the burning embers.

"Be of good heart," said Taluta, at last, "for you shall meet my twin spirit! She will love you as I do, and you will love her as you love me. This was our covenant before we came into this world."

The conception of a "twin spirit" was familiar to the Sioux. "Ho," responded the warrior, with dignity and all seriousness. He felt a great awe for the spirit, and dared not lift his eyes to her face.

"Weep no more, kechuwa, weep no more," she softly added; and the next moment Antelope found himself outside the mysterious teepee. His limbs were stiff and cold, but he did not feel faint nor hungry. Having filled his pipe, he held it up to the spirits and then partook of the smoke; and thus revived, he slowly and reluctantly left the sacred spot.

The main war-party also visited the old camp and saw the solitary teepee grave, but did not linger there. They continued on the trail of the caravan until they reached the new camping ground. They called themselves successful, although they had left several of their number on the field. Their triumph songs indicated this; therefore the people hurried to receive the news and to learn who were the unfortunates.

The father of Antelope was foremost among those who ran to meet the war-party. He learned that his son had distinguished himself in the fight, and that his name was not mentioned among the brave dead.

"And where, then, is he?" he asked, with unconcealed anxiety.

"He left us three days ago to come in advance," they replied.

"But he has not arrived!" exclaimed old Wezee, in much agitation.

He returned to his teepee, where he consoled himself as best he could by smoking the pipe in solitude. He could neither sing praises nor indulge in the death dirge, and none came in either to congratulate or mourn with him.

The sun had disappeared behind the hills, and the old man still sat gazing into the burning embers, when he heard a horse's footfall at the door of his lodge.

"Ho, atay (father)!" came the welcome call.

"Mechinkshe! mechinkshe!" (my son, my son), he replied in unrestrained joy. Old We-zee now stood on the threshold and sang the praise song for his son, ending with a war-whoop such as he had not indulged in since he was quite a young man.

The camp was once more alive with the dances, and the dull thud of the Indian drum was continually in the air. The council had agreed that Antelope was entitled to wear a war-bonnet of eagles' feathers. He was accordingly summoned before the aboriginal parliament, and from the wise men of the tribe he received his degree of war-bonnet.

It was a public ceremony. The great pipe was held up for him to take the smoke of high honor.

The happiest person present was the father of Antelope; but he himself remained calm and unmoved throughout the ceremony.

"He is a strange person," was the whisper among a group of youths who were watching the proceedings with envious eyes.

The young man was strangely listless and depressed in spirit. His old grandmother knew why, but none of the others understood. He never joined in the village festivities, while the rest of his family were untiring in the dances, and old Wezee was at the height of his happiness.

It was a crisp October morning, and the family were eating their breakfast of broiled bison meat, when the large drum at the council lodge was struck three times. The old man set down his wooden basin.

"Ah, my son, the war-chiefs will make an announcement! It may be a call for the enlistment of warriors! I am sorry," he said, and paused. "I am sorry, because I would rather no war-party went out at present. I am getting old. I have enjoyed your success, my son. I love to hear the people speak your name. If you go again upon the war-path, I shall no longer be able to join in the celebrations. Something tells me that you will not return!"

Young braves were already on their way to the council lodge. Tatoka looked, and the temptation was great.

"Father, it is not becoming for me to remain at home when others go," he said, at last.

"Ho," was the assent uttered by the father, with a deep sigh.

"Five hundred braves have enlisted to go with the great war prophet against the three confederated tribes," he afterward reported at home, with an air of elation which he had not worn for some moons.

Since Antelope had received the degree of war-bonnet, his father had spared neither time nor his meager means in his behalf. He had bartered his most cherished possessions for several eagles that were brought in by various hunters of the camp, and with his own hands had made a handsome war-bonnet for his son.

"You will now wear a war-bonnet for the first time, and you are the first of our family who has earned the right to wear one for many generations. I am proud of you, my son," he said as he presented it.

But when the youth replied : " Ho, ho, father! I ought to be a brave man in recognition of this honor," he again sighed heavily.

" It is that I feared, my son! Many a young man has lost his life for vanity and love of display! "

The evening serenades began early, for the party was to leave at once. In groups upon their favorite ponies the warriors rode around the inner circle of the great camp, singing their war-songs. All the people came out of the tee-pees, and sitting by twos and threes upon the ground, bedecked with savage finery, they watched and listened. The pretty wild maidens had this last opportunity given them to look upon the faces of their sweethearts, whom they might never see again. Here and there an old man was singing the gratitude song or thank-offering, while announcing the first war-path of a novice, for such an announcement meant the giving of many presents to the poor and aged. So the camp was filled with songs of joy and pride in the departing husbands, brothers, and sons.

As soon as darkness set in the sound of the rude native flute was added to the celebration. This is the lover's farewell. The young braves, wrapped from head to foot in their finest robes, each sounded the plaintive strains near the tee-pee of the beloved. The playful yodeling of many voices in chorus was heard at the close of each song.

At midnight the army of five hundred, the flower of the Sioux, marched against their ancient enemy. Antelope was in the best of spirits. He had his war-bonnet to display before the enemy! He was now regarded as one of the foremost warriors of his band, and might probably be asked to perform some specially hazardous duty, so that he was fully prepared to earn further distinction.

In five days the Sioux were encamped within a day's travel of the permanent village of the confederated tribes—the Rees, Mandans, and Gros Ventres. The war-chief selected two men, Antelope and Eaglechild, to scout at night

in advance of the main force. It was thought
that most of the hunters had already returned
to their winter quarters, and in this case the
Sioux would have no mean enemy to face. On
the other hand, a battle was promised that
would enlarge their important traditions.

The two made their way as rapidly as possible toward the ancestral home of their enemies. It was a night perfectly suited to what
they had to do, for the moon was full, the
fleeting clouds hiding it from time to time and
casting deceptive shadows.

When they had come within a short distance
of the lodges unperceived, they lay flat for a
long time, and studied the ways of the young
men in every particular, for it was Antelope's
plan to enter the great village and mingle
boldly with its inhabitants. Even their hoots and
love-calls were carefully noted, so that they
might be able to imitate them. There were
several entertainments in progress in different
parts of the village, yet it was apparent that
the greatest vigilance was observed. The
lodges of poles covered with earth were partly

underground, and at one end the war-horses were stabled, as a precaution against a possible surprise.

At the moment that a large cloud floated over the moon, casting a shadow large enough to cover the entire village, the drum in one of the principal lodges was struck in quick time, accompanied by boisterous war-whoops and singing. The two scouts adjusted their robes about them in the fashion of the strangers, and walked openly in that direction.

They glanced quickly from side to side as they approached, but no one paid any attention, so they came up with other young men and peeped through the chinks in the earth wigwam. It was a great gambling party. Among the guests were several distinguished warriors, and each at an opportune time would rise and recount his great deeds in warfare against the Sioux. The strangers could read their gestures, and Antelope was once or twice almost on the point of stringing his bow to send an arrow through the audacious speaker.

As they moved about the village, taking note

of its numbers and situation, and waiting an opportunity to withdraw without exciting suspicion, they observed some of the younger braves standing near another large wigwam, and one or two even peeped within. Moved by sudden curiosity, Antelope followed their example. He uttered a low exclamation and at once withdrew.

"What is it?" asked his companion, but received no answer.

It was evidently the home of a chief. The family were seated within at their usual occupations, and the bright light of the central fire shone full upon the face of a most lovely maiden.

Antelope stood apparently motionless, but he was trembling under his robe like a leaf.

"Come, friend, there is another large cloud almost over the moon! We must move away under its concealing shadow," urged Eagle-child.

The other stood still as if undecided, but at last he approached the lodge and looked in a second time. There sat his sweetheart in human form once more! The maiden was attired in a doeskin gown set with elk's teeth like ivory. Her eyes were cast down demurely over her embroidery, but in every feature she was the living counterpart of Taluta!

At last the two got away unobserved, and hastened toward the place where they had concealed their horses. But here Antelope sent his companion on in advance, making the excuse that he wished to study further the best position from which to make the attack.

When he was left alone he stood still for a moment to decide upon a plan. He could think of nothing but that he must meet the Ree maiden before daylight! He realized the extreme hazard of the attempt, but he also recalled what he had been told by the spirit of Taluta, and the supernatural command seemed to justify him even in going thus upon the eve of battle to meet the enemy of his people.

He skirted the heavy timber and retraced his steps to a point from which he could see the village. The drum of the gambling party had ceased with the shouts and laughter of the players. Apparently the village was lost in slumber. The moon had set, and without pausing he advanced to the home of the girl. As he came near some dogs began to bark, but he silenced them after the manner of the Rees, and they obeyed him.

When Antelope softly raised the robe that hung over the entrance to the chief's lodge, he saw the fire smoldering in the center, and the members of the household lying in their respective places, all seemingly in a deep sleep. The girl lay opposite the entrance, where he had seen her seated in the early part of the evening.

The heart of the Sioux beat violently, and he glanced nervously to left and right. There was neither sound nor movement. Then he pulled his robe completely over his head, after the fashion of a Ree lover, and softly entered the wigwam.

The Ree maiden, having industriously worked on her embroidery until far into the night, had retired to rest. In her dreams, the twin sister came to her of whom she had had visions ever since she could remember, and especially when something of importance was about to happen.

This time she came with a handsome young man of another tribe, and said: " Sister, I bring you a Sioux, who will be your husband! "

The dreamer opened her eyes to behold a youth bending over her and gently pulling her robe, as a suitor is permitted to do to awaken his beloved.

When he saw that she was awake, the Sioux touched his breast, saying in a whisper, " Tatoka," and made the sign for Antelope. This pleased the Ree girl, for her own brother, who had died the year before, had borne that name. She immediately sat up and stirred the embers into a light blaze. Then she took hold of his blanket and drew it from his face; and there she seemed to see the very features of the man of her vision!

He took her hand in his, and she felt the force of love stream through his long, nervous fingers, and instinctively knew his thoughts. In her turn she touched her breast and made the sign for Shield, pronouncing in her own tongue the word, Stasu. This seemed to him also a name of good omen, and in the sign language which was common to all the people of the plains, he asked her to be his wife.

Vividly her dream came back to her, and she could not refuse the stranger. Her soul already responded to his; and for a few minutes they sat silently side by side. When he arose and beckoned, "Come with me," she had no question to make, and without a word she followed him from her father's lodge and out into the forest.

In the midst of his ascending fame, at a moment when opportunity seemed to favor his ambition, the brave Antelope had mysteriously disappeared! His companion scout returned with a favorable report. He said that the men of the three confederated tribes were gambling and feasting, wholly unconscious of danger, and that Antelope would follow him with a further report upon the best point of attack.

The red warriors impatiently awaited his return, until it became apparent that they could wait no longer without sacrificing their chance of success. When the attack was made it was already rather late. The sun had fairly cleared the eastern hills, and most of the men were outside their lodges.

It was a great battle! Again and again the Sioux were repulsed, but as often they rallied and repeated the charge until sundown, when they effected their retreat with considerable loss. Had Antelope returned in due season, the charge would have been made before dawn, while the people were yet asleep.

When the battle was over, the Rees, Mandans, and Gros Ventres gathered their dead and wounded. The night was filled with mourning. Soon the sad news was heralded throughout the camp that the beautiful daughter of the Ree chief was among the missing. It was supposed that she must have been captured while driving her ponies to water in the early morning. The grief for her loss was mingled with horror, because of a fear that she might suffer humiliation at the hands of the Sioux war-

riors, and among the young men there were muttered threats that the Sioux would pay dearly
for this.

Though partially successful, the Sioux had
lost many of their bravest warriors, and none
could tell what had happened to Antelope—he
who had been believed the favorite of the gods
of war. It was suggested by some envious ones
that perhaps he had recognized the strongly
entrenched position of the three tribes, and be-
lieving the battle would be a disastrous one,
had set out for home without making his report. But this supposition was not deemed
credible. On the other hand, the idea was entertained that he had reëntered the village, was
detected and slain; and therefore the enemy
was on the lookout when the attack was made.

" Hay, hay, hay, mechinkshe (Alas, alas,
my son) ! " was the sorrowful cry with which
his old father received the news. His head
fell upon his breast, and all the others groaned
in sympathy.

The sunset sky was a blanket of beautiful
painting. There were camp-fires among the

clouds in orange and scarlet, while some were black as night. So the camp fairly glowed in celebration of its heroes; yet there was deep grief in many families. When the evening meal had been eaten and the people were sitting outside their lodges, a tall old man, almost nude, appeared in the circle, riding a fine horse. He had blackened his face, his hair was cut short, and the horse also had been deprived of his flowing mane and tail. Both were in deep mourning, after the fashion of the Sioux.

"Ho, ho!" exclaimed many warriors as he passed them, singing in a hoarse, guttural voice.

"Ugh, he sings a war-song!" remarked one.

"Yes, I am told that he will find his son's bones, or leave his own in the country of the enemy!"

The rain had fallen incessantly for two days. The fleeing lovers had reached this lonely mountain valley of the Big Horn region on the night that the cold fall rains set in, and Antelope had hurriedly constructed an arbor house or rude shelter of pine and cedar boughs.

THE LOVE OF ANTELOPE

It was enough. There they sat, man and
wife, in their first home of living green! The
cheerful fire was burning in the center, and the
happy smoke went straight up among the tall
pines. There was no human eye to gaze upon
them to embarrass—not even a common language in which to express their love for one
another.

Their marriage, they believed, was made by
a spirit, and it was holy in their minds. Each
had cast away his people and his all for the
sake of this emotion which had suddenly overtaken them both with overwhelming force, and
the warrior's ambition had disappeared before
it like a morning mist before the sun.

To them a new life was just beginning, and
they had all but forgotten the existence of any
world save this. The young bride was en-
shrined in a bower of spicy fragrance, and her
face shone whenever her eyes met those of her
husband.

"This is as I would have it, kechuwa (darling)!" exclaimed the Sioux in his own language. She simply responded with a childlike

[51]

smile. Although she did not understand his words, she read in the tones of his voice only happy and loving thoughts.

The Ree girl had prepared a broiled bison steak, and her husband was keeping the fire well fed with dry fagots. The odor of the burning fat was delicious, and the gentle patter of the rain made a weird music outside their wigwam.

As soon as her husband had left her alone —for he must go to water the ponies and conceal them at a distance—Stasu came out to collect more wood. Instinctively she looked all about her. Huge mountains towered skyward, clad in pines. The narrow valley in which she was wound its way between them, and on every side there was heavy forest.

She stood silent and awed, scarcely able to realize that she had begun her new life absolutely alone, with no other woman to advise or congratulate her, and visited only by the birds of the air. Yet all the world to her just now was Antelope! No other woman could smile on him. He could not talk to any one but her. The evening drum at the council lodge could not summon him away from her, and she was well content.

When the young wife had done everything she could think of in preparation for her husband's return, including the making of several birch-bark basins and pails for water, the rain had quite ceased, so she spread her robe just outside the lodge and took up her work-bag, in which she had several pairs of moccasin-tops already beaded.

While she bent over her work, getting up from time to time to turn the roast which she had impaled upon a sharp stick above the glowing coals, the bride had a stream of shy callers, of the little people of the woods. She sat very still, so as not to startle them, and there is much curiosity among these people concerning a stranger.

Presently she was startled by a footfall not unlike that of a man. She had not been married long enough to know the sound of her husband's step, and she felt a thrill of joy and fear alternately. It might be he, and it might be a stranger! She was loath to look up, but at last gave a furtive glance, and met squarely the eyes of a large grizzly bear, who was seated upon his haunches not far away.

Stasu was surprised, but she showed no fear; and fearlessness is the best shield against wild animals. In a moment she got up unconcernedly, and threw a large piece of meat to the stranger.

" Take of my wedding feast, O great Bear! " she addressed him, " and be good to me to bless my first teepee! O be kind and recognize my brave act in taking for my husband one of the warriors of the Sioux, the ancient enemy of my people! I have accepted a husband of a language other than mine, and am come to live among you as your neighbor. I offer you my friendship! "

The bear's only answer to her prayer was a low growl, but having eaten the meat, he turned and clumsily departed.

In the meantime Antelope had set himself to master the geography of that region, to study the outlook for game, and ascertain the best approaches to their secret home. It was already settled in his mind that he could never return either to his wife's people or to his own. His fellow-warriors would not forgive his desertion, and the Rees could not be expected to welcome as a kinsman one of the foremost of their ancient foes. There was nothing to be done but to remain in seclusion, and let them say what they would of him!

He had loved the Ree maiden from the first moment he beheld her by the light of the blazing embers, and that love must satisfy him. It was well that he had never cared much for company, but had spent many of his young days in solitude and fasting. It did not seem at all strange to him that he had been forced to retreat into an unknown and wild country with a woman whom he saw in the evening for the first time, and fled with as his own wife before sunrise!

By the afternoon he had thoroughly informed himself upon the nature of the surrounding country. Everything on the face of the map was surveyed and charted in his mind, in accordance with his habits and training. This done, he turned toward his secret dwelling. As he walked rapidly and noiselessly through the hidden valleys and along the singing streams, he noticed fresh signs of the deer, elk, and other wild tribes among whom he had chosen to abide. " They shall be my people," he said to himself.

Behind a group of cedars he paused to reconnoiter, and saw the pine-bough wigwam like a giant plant, each row of boughs overlapping the preceding circular row like the scales of a fish. Stasu was sitting before it upon a buffalo-robe, attired in her best doeskin gown. Her delicate oval face was touched with red paint, and her slender brown hands were occupied with a moccasin meant for him to wear. He could scarcely believe that it was a mortal woman that he saw before him in broad day —the pride of No Man's Trail, for that is what the Crow Indians call that valley!

" Ho, ho, kechuwa! " he exclaimed as he approached her, and her heart leaped in recognition of the magnetic words of love.

THE LOVE OF ANTELOPE

" It is good that we are alone! I shall never want to go back to my people so long as I have you. I can dwell here with you forever, unless you should think otherwise!" she exclaimed in her own tongue, accompanied by graphic signs.

" Ho, I think of nothing else! I can see in every creature only friendly ways and good feeling. We can live alone here, happily, unless you should feel differently," he replied in his own language with the signs, so that his bride understood him.

The environment was just what it should be when two people are united in marriage. The wedding music was played by Nature, and trees, brooks, and the birds of the air contributed their peculiar strains to a great harmony. All of the people on No Man's Trail were polite, and understood the reserves of love. These two had yielded to a simple and natural impulse; but its only justification to their minds was the mysterious leading of the twin spirit! That was the sum total of their excuse, and it was enough.

Before the rigor of winter had set in, Tatoka brought to his bride many buffalo skins. She was thoroughly schooled in the arts of savage womanhood; in fact, every Indian maid was trained with this thought in view—that she should become a beautiful, strong, skillful wife and mother—the mother of a noble race of warriors!

In a short time within that green and pine-scented enclosure there smiled a little wild paradise. Hard by the pine-bough wigwam there stood a new white buffalo-skin teepee, tanned, cut, sewed, and pitched by the hands of Stasu. Away in the woods, down by the rushing brook, was her tannery, and not far away, in a sunny, open spot, she prepared her sun-cured meats for winter use. Her kitchen was a stone fireplace in a shady spot, and her parlor was the lodge of evergreen, overhung on two sides by inaccessible ledges, and bounded on the other two by the sparkling stream. It was a secret place, and yet a citadel; a silent place, and yet not lonely!

The winter was cold and long, but the pair

were happy in one another's company, and accepted their strange lot as one that was chosen for them by the spirits. Stasu had insisted upon her husband speaking to her in his own language, that she might learn it quickly. In a little while she was able to converse with him, and when she had acquired his language she taught him hers.

While Antelope was occupied with hunting and exploring the country, always keeping in mind the danger of discovery by some wandering scout or hunter, his wife grew well acquainted with the wild inhabitants of No Man's Trail. These people are as full of curiosity as man, and as the Sioux never hunted near his home, they were entirely fearless. Many came to the door of Stasu's lodge, and she was not afraid, but offered them food and spoke to them kindly. All animals judge by signs and are quick in reading tones and gestures; so that the Ree girl soon had grandfathers and grandmothers, after the Indian fashion, among the wolves and bears that came oftenest for food.

Her husband in the field had also his fellow-hunters and friends. When he killed the buffalo he always left enough meat for the wolves, the eagles, and the ravens to feast upon, and these watched for the coming of the lonely wild man. More than once they told him by their actions of the presence of a distant camp-fire, but in each instance it proved to be a small war-party which had passed below them on the trail.

Again it was summer. Never had the mountains looked grander or more mysterious to the eyes of the two. The valley was full of the music and happiness of the winged summer people; the trees wore their summer attire, and the meadow its green blanket. There were many homes made happy by the coming of little people everywhere, but no pair was happier than Stasu and her husband when one morning they saw their little brave lying wrapped in soft deerskins, and heard for the first time his plaintive voice!

That morning, when Antelope set out on the hunt, he stopped at the stream and looked at

himself seriously to see whether he had changed
since the day before. He must now appear
much graver, he said to himself, because he is
the father of a new man!

In spite of himself, his thoughts were with
his own people, and he wondered what his old
grandmother would have said to his child! He
looked away off toward the Black Hills, to the
Sioux country, and in his heart he said, "I am
a coward!"

The boy grew naturally, and never felt the
lack of playmates and companions, for his
mother was ingenious in devising plays for
him, and in winning for him the confidence and
kindness of the animal friends. He was the
young chief and the hero of No Man's Trail!
The bears and wolves were his warriors; the
buffalo and elk the hostile tribes upon whom he
went to war. Small as he was, he soon preferred to roam alone in the woods. His parents were often anxious, but, on the other hand,
they entertained the hope that he would some
day be "wakan," a mysterious or supernatural
man, for he was getting power from his wild

companions and from the silent forces of nature.

One day, when he was about five years old, he gave a dance for his wild pets upon the little plateau which was still their home. He had clothed Mato, the bear, in one of his father's suits as a great medicine-man. Waho, the wolf, was painted up as a brave; and the young buffalo calf was attired in one of his mother's gowns. The boy acted as chief and master of ceremonies.

The savage mother watched him with undisguised pride, mingled with sorrow. Tears coursed down her dusky cheeks, although at the same time she could not help laughing heartily at the strange performance. When the play was ended, and she had served the feast at its close, Stasu seemed lost in thought.

"He should not live in this way," she was saying to herself. "He should know the traditions and great deeds of my people! Surely his grandfather would be proud of the boy!"

That evening, while the boy slept, and Mato lay outside the lodge eagerly listening and sniffing the night air, the parents sat silent and ill at ease. After a long time Stasu spoke her mind.

"My husband, you ask me why I am sad. It is because I think that the Great Mystery will be displeased if we keep this little boy forever in the wilderness. It is wrong to allow him to grow up among wild animals; and if sickness or accident should deprive him of his father and mother, our spirits would never rest, because we had left him alone! I have decided to ask you to take us back, either to your people or to my people. We must sacrifice our pride, or, if needs be, our lives, for his life and happiness!"

This speech of Stasu's was a surprise to her husband. His eyes rested upon the ground as he listened, and his face assumed the proverbial stoical aspect, yet in it there was not lacking a certain nobleness. At last he lifted his eyes to hers, and said:

"You have spoken wise words, and it shall be as you have said. We shall return to your people. If I am to die at the hands of the an-

cient enemy of the Sioux, I shall die because
of my love for you, and for our child. But I
cannot go back to my own people to be ridiculed
by unworthy young men for yielding to love of
a Ree maiden!"

There was much feeling behind these words
of Antelope. The rigid customs of his people
are almost a religion, and there is one thing
above all else which a Sioux cannot bear—that
is the ridicule of his fellow-warriors. Yes,
he can endure severe punishment or even death
at the hands of the enemy rather than a single
laugh of derision from a Sioux!

In a few days the houshold articles were
packed, and the three sadly turned their backs
upon their home. Stasu and her husband were
very silent as they traveled slowly along. When
they reached the hill called "Born-of-Day,"
and she saw from its summit the country of her
people lying below her, she cried aloud, weeping happy tears. Antelope sat near by with
bowed head, silently smoking.

Finally on the fifth day they arrived within
sight of the great permanent village of the

three tribes. They saw the earth lodges as of old, thickly clustered along the flats of the Missouri, among their rustling maize-fields. Antelope stopped. " I think you had better give me something to eat, woman," he said, smiling. It was the Sioux way of saying, " Let me have my last meal! "

After they had eaten, Stasu opened her buckskin bags and gave her husband his finest suit. He dressed himself carefully in the fashion of his tribe, putting on all the feathers to which he was entitled as a warrior. The boy also was decked out in gala attire, and Stasu, the matron, had never looked more beautiful in her gown of ceremony with the decoration of elks' teeth, the same that she had worn on the evening of her disappearance.

As she dressed herself, the unwelcome thought forced itself upon her,—" What if my love is killed by my own countrymen in their frenzy? This beautiful gown must then give place to a poor one, and this hair will be cut short! " for such is the mourning of the widow among her people.

The three rode openly down the long slope, and were instantly discovered by the people of the village. Soon the plain was black with the approaching riders. Stasu had begged her husband to remain behind, while she went on alone with the boy to obtain forgiveness, but he sternly refused, and continued in advance. When the foremost Ree warriors came within arrow-shot they began to shoot, to which he paid no attention.

But the child screamed with terror, and Stasu cried out in her own tongue:

" Do not shoot! I am the daughter of your chief!"

One of them returned the reply: " She is killed by the Sioux!" But when the leaders saw her plainly they were astounded.

For a time there was great confusion. Some held that they should all die, for the woman had been guilty of treason to her people, and even now she might be playing a trick upon them. Who could say that behind that hill there was not a Sioux war-party?

" No, no," replied others. " They are in our power. Let them tell their story!"

Stasu told it simply, and said in conclusion:

"This man, one of the bravest and most honorable men of his tribe, deserted on the night of the attack, and all because he loved a Ree maiden! He now comes to be your brother-in-law, who will fight henceforth for you and with you, even if it be against his own people.

"He does not beg for mercy—he can dare anything! But I am a woman—my heart is soft—I ask for the lives of my husband and my son, who is the grandson of your chief!"

"He is a coward who touches this man!" exclaimed the leader, and a thunder of war-whoops went up in approval of his words.

The warriors formed themselves in two great columns, riding twenty abreast, behind and in front of the strangers. The old chief came out to meet them, and took his son-in-law's hand. Thus they entered the village in battle array, but with hearts touched with wonder and great gladness, discharging their arrows upward in clouds and singing peace-songs.

II

THE MADNESS OF BALD EAGLE

I T was many years ago, when I was only a child," began White Ghost, the patriarchal old chief of the Yanktonnais Sioux, "that our band was engaged in a desperate battle with the Rees and Mandans. The cause of the fight was a peculiar one. I will tell you about it." And he laid aside his long-stemmed pipe and settled himself to the recital.

"At that time the Yanktonnais numbered a little over forty families. We were nicknamed by the other bands Shunkikcheka, or Domestic Dogs, because of our owning large numbers of these animals. My father was the head chief.

"Our favorite wintering place was a timbered tract near the mouth of the Grand River, and it was here that we met the Blackfoot Sioux in the fall hunt. On the opposite side of the river from our camp was the permanent village of the Rees and Mandans, whose houses were of dirt and partly underground. For a hundred years before this time they had planted large gardens, and we were accustomed to buy of them corn, beans, and pumpkins. From time to time our people had made treaties of peace with them. Each family of the Rees had one or two buffalo boats—not round, as the Sioux made them, but two or three skins long. In these boats they brought quantities of dried beans and other vegetables to trade with us for jerked buffalo meat.

" It was a great gathering and a time of general festivity and hospitality. The Sioux young men were courting the Ree girls, and the Ree braves were courting our girls, while the old people bartered their produce. All day the river was alive with canoes and its banks rang with the laughter of the youths and maidens.

" My father's younger brother, whose name was Big Whip, had a close friend, a young man who ever after the event of which I am about to tell you was known as Bald Eagle. They were both daring young men and very ambitious for distinction. They had been following the

Ree girls to their canoes as they returned to their homes in the evening.

"Big Whip and his friend stood upon the river bank at sunset, one with a quiver full of arrows upon his back while the other carried a gun under his blanket. Nearly all the people of the other village had crossed the river, and the chief of the Rees, whose name was Bald Eagle, went home with his wife last of all. It was about dusk as they entered their bullhide boat, and the two Sioux stood there looking at them.

"Suddenly Big Whip exclaimed: 'Friend, let us kill the chief. I dare you to kill and scalp him!' His friend replied:

"'It shall be as you say. I will stand by you in all things. I am willing to die with you.'

"Accordingly Bald Eagle pulled out his gun and shot the Ree dead. From that day he took his name. The old man fell backward into his boat, and the old woman screamed and wept as she rowed him across the river. The other young man shot an arrow or two at the wife, but she continued to row until she reached the other bank.

"There was great excitement on both sides of the river as soon as the people saw what had happened. There were two camps of Sioux, the Blackfoot Sioux and the Yanktonnais, or our people. Of course the Mandans and Rees greatly outnumbered us; their camp must have numbered two or three thousand, which was more than we had in our combined camps.

"There was a Sioux whose name was Black Shield, who had intermarried among the Rees. He came down to the opposite bank of the Missouri and shouted to us:

"'Of which one of your bands is the man who killed Bald Eagle?'

"One of the Blackfoot Sioux replied:

"'It is a man of the Yanktonnais Sioux who killed Bald Eagle.'

"Then he said: 'The Rees wish to do battle with them; you had better withdraw from their camp.'

"Accordingly the Blackfeet retired about a mile from us upon the bluffs and pitched their tents, while the Yanktonnais remained on the flats. The two bands had been great rivals in courage and the art of war, so we did not ask for help from our kinsfolk, but during the night we dug trenches about the camp, the inner one for the women and children, and the outer one for the men to stay in and do battle.

"The next morning at daybreak the enemy landed and approached our camp in great numbers. Some of their women and old men came also, and sat upon the bluffs to watch the fight and to carry off their dead and wounded. The Blackfeet likewise were watching the battle from the bluffs, and just before the fight began one Blackfoot came in with his wife and joined us. His name was Red Dog's Track, but from that day he was called He-Came-Back. His wife was a Yanktonnais, and he had said to her: 'If I don't join your tribe to-day, my brothers-in-law will call me a coward.'

"The Sioux were well entrenched and well armed with guns and arrows, and their aim was deadly, so that the Rees crawled up gradually and took every opportunity to pick off any

Sioux who ventured to show his head above the trenches. In like manner every Ree who exposed himself was sure to die.

"Up to this time no one had seen the two men who made all the trouble. There was a natural hollow in the bank, concealed by buffalo berry bushes, very near where they stood when Bald Eagle shot the Ree.

"'Friend,' said Big Whip, 'it is likely that our own people will punish us for this deed. They will pursue and kill us wherever they find us. They have the right to do this. The best thing is to drop into this washout and remain there until they cease to look for us.'

"They did so, and remained hidden during the night. But, after the fight began, Big Whip said again: 'Friend, we are the cause of the deaths of many brave men this day. We committed the act to show our bravery. We dared each other to do it. It will now become us as warriors to join our band.'

"They both stripped, and taking their weapons in hand, ran toward the camp. They had to pass directly through the enemy's lines, but they were not recognized till they had fairly passed them. Then they were between two fires. When they had almost reached the entrenchment they faced about and fired at the Rees, jumping about incessantly to avoid being hit, as is the Indian fashion. Bullets and arrows were flying all about them like hail, but at last they dropped back unhurt into the Sioux trenches. Thus the two men saved their reputation for bravery, and their people never openly reproached them for the events of that day. Young men are often rash, but it is not well to reprove one for a brave deed lest he become a coward.

"Many were killed, but more of the Rees than of our band. About the middle of the afternoon there came a cold rain. It was in the fall of the year. The bow-strings were wet, and the guns were only flint-locks. You know when the flint becomes wet it is useless, and it looked as if the fight must be with knives.

"But the Rees were much disheartened. They had lost many. The women were all the time carrying off the wounded, and there were the Blackfoot Sioux watching them from the hills. They turned and fled toward the river. The Sioux followed like crazy wolves, tomahawking the tired and slow ones. Many were killed at the boats, and some of the boats were punctured with shot and sank. Some carried a load of Sioux arrows back across the river. That was the greatest battle ever fought by our band," the old man concluded, with a deep sigh of mingled satisfaction and regret.

III

THE SINGING SPIRIT

I

"HO my steed, we must climb one more hill! My reputation depends upon my report!"

Anookasan addressed his pony as if he were a human companion, urged on like himself by human need and human ambition. And yet in his heart he had very little hope of sighting any buffalo in that region at just that time of the year.

The Yankton Sioux were ordinarily the most far-sighted of their people in selecting a winter camp, but this year the late fall had caught them rather far east of the Missouri bottoms, their favorite camping-ground. The upper Jim River, called by the Sioux the River of Gray Woods, was usually bare of large game at that season. Their store of jerked buffalo meat did not hold out as they had hoped, and by March it became an urgent necessity to send out scouts for buffalo.

The old men at the tiyo teepee (council lodge) held a long council. It was decided to select ten of their bravest and hardiest young men to explore the country within three days' journey of their camp.

" Anookasan, uyeyo-o-o, woo, woo! " Thus the ten men were summoned to the council lodge early in the evening to receive their commission. Anookasan was the first called and first to cross the circle of the teepees. A young man of some thirty years, of the original native type, his massive form was wrapped in a fine buffalo robe with the hair inside. He wore a stately eagle feather in his scalp-lock, but no paint about his face.

As he entered the lodge all the inmates greeted him with marked respect, and he was given the place of honor. When all were seated the great drum was struck and a song sung by four deep-chested men. This was the prelude to a peculiar ceremony.

A large red pipe, which had been filled and

laid carefully upon the central hearth, was now taken up by an old man, whose face was painted red. First he held it to the ground with the words: "Great Mother, partake of this!" Then he held it toward the sky, saying: "Great Father, smoke this!" Finally he lighted it, took four puffs, pointing it to the four corners of the earth in turn, and lastly presented it to Anookasan. This was the oath of office, administered by the chief of the council lodge. The other nine were similarly commissioned, and all accepted the appointment.

It was no light task that was thus religiously enjoined upon these ten men. It meant at the least several days and nights of wandering in search of signs of the wily buffalo. It was a public duty, and a personal one as well; one that must involve untold hardship; and if overtaken by storm the messengers were in peril of death!

Anookasan returned to his teepee with some misgiving. His old charger, which had so often carried him to victory, was not so strong as he had been in his prime. As his master approached the lodge the old horse welcomed him with a gentle whinny. He was always tethered near by, ready for any emergency.

" Ah, Wakan! we are once more called upon to do duty! We shall set out before day-break."

As he spoke, he pushed nearer a few strips of the poplar bark, which was oats to the Indian pony of the olden time.

Anookasan had his extra pair of buffalo-skin moccasins with the hair inside, and his scanty provision of dried meat neatly done up in a small packet and fastened to his saddle. With his companions he started northward, up the River of the Gray Woods, five on the east side and a like number on the west.

The party had separated each morning, so as to cover as much ground as possible, having agreed to return at night to the river. It was now the third day; their food was all but gone, their steeds much worn, and the signs seemed to indicate a storm. Yet the hunger of their friends and their own pride impelled them to persist, for out of many young men they had

[79]

been chosen, therefore they must prove themselves equal to the occasion.

The sun, now well toward the western horizon, cast over snow-covered plains a purplish light. No living creature was in sight and the quest seemed hopeless, but Anookasan was not one to accept defeat.

"There may be an outlook from yonder hill which will turn failure into success," he thought, as he dug his heels into the sides of his faithful nag. At the same time he started a "Strong Heart" song to keep his courage up!

At the summit of the ascent he paused and gazed steadily before him. At the foot of the next coteau he beheld a strip of black. He strained his eyes to look, for the sun had already set behind the hilltops. It was a great herd of buffaloes, he thought, which was grazing on the foot-hills.

"Hi, hi, uncheedah! Hi, hi, tunkasheedah!" he was about to exclaim in gratitude, when, looking more closely, he discovered his mistake. The dark patch was only timber.

His horse could not carry him any further,

so he got off and ran behind him toward the river. At dusk he hailed his companions.

" Ho, what success? " one cried.

" Not a sign of even a lone bull," replied another.

" Yet I saw a gray wolf going north this evening. His direction is propitious," remarked Anookasan, as he led the others down the slope and into the heavy timber. The river just here made a sharp turn, forming a densely wooded semicircle, in the shelter of a high bluff.

The braves were all downhearted because of their ill-luck, and only the sanguine spirit of Anookasan kept them from utter discouragement. Their slight repast had been taken and each man had provided himself with abundance of dry grass and twigs for a bed. They had built a temporary wigwam of the same material, in the center of which there was a generous fire. Each man stretched himself out upon his robe in the glow of it. Anookasan filled the red pipe, and, having lighted it, he took one or two hasty puffs and held it up to the moon, which was scarcely visible behind the cold clouds.

"Great Mother, partake of this smoke! May I eat meat to-morrow!" he exclaimed with solemnity. Having uttered this prayer, he handed the pipe to the man nearest him.

For a time they all smoked in silence; then came a distant call.

"Ah, it is Shunkmanito, the wolf! There is something cheering in his voice to-night," declared Anookasan. "Yes, I am sure he is telling us not to be discouraged. You know that the wolf is one of our best friends in trouble. Many a one has been guided back to his home by him in a blizzard, or led to game when in desperate need. My friends, let us not turn back in the morning; let us go north one more day!"

No one answered immediately, and again silence reigned, while one by one they pulled the reluctant whiffs of smoke through the long stem of the calumet.

"What is that?" said one of the men, and all listened intently to catch the delicate sound.

They were familiar with all the noises of the night and voices of the forest, but this was not like any of them.

"It sounds like the song of a mosquito, and one might forget while he listens that this is not midsummer," said one.

"I hear also the medicine-man's single drum-beat," suggested another.

"There is a tradition," remarked Anookasan, "that many years ago a party of hunters went up the river on a scout like this of ours. They never returned. Afterward, in the summer, their bones were found near the home of a strange creature, said to be a little man, but he had hair all over him. The Isantees call him Chanotedah. Our old men give him the name Oglugechana. This singular being is said to be no larger than a new-born babe. He speaks an unknown tongue.

"The home of Oglugechana is usually a hollow stump, around which all of the nearest trees are felled by lightning. There is an open spot in the deep woods wherever he dwells. His weapons are the plumes of various birds. Great

[83]

numbers of these variegated feathers are to be found in the deserted lodge of the little man.

" It is told by the old men that Oglugechana has a weird music by which he sometimes bewitches lone travelers. He leads them hither and thither about his place until they have lost their senses. Then he speaks to them. He may make of them great war-prophets or medicine-men, but his commands are hard to fulfill. If any one sees him and comes away before he is bewildered, the man dies as soon as he smells the camp-fire, or when he enters his home his nearest relative dies suddenly."

The warrior who related this legend assumed the air of one who narrates authentic history, and his listeners appeared to be seriously impressed. What we call the supernatural was as real to them as any part of their lives.

" This thing does not stop to breathe at all. His music seems to go on endlessly," said one, with considerable uneasiness.

" It comes from the heavy timber north of us, under the high cliff," reported a warrior who had stepped outside of the rude temporary structure to inform himself more clearly of the direction of the sound.

"Anookasan, you are our leader—tell us what we should do! We will follow you. ' I believe we ought to leave this spot immediately. This is perhaps the spirit of some dead enemy," suggested another. Meanwhile, the red pipe was refilled and sent around the circle to calm their disturbed spirits.

When the calumet returned at last to the one addressed, he took it in a preoccupied manner, and spoke between labored pulls on the stem.

"I am just like yourselves—nothing more than flesh—with a spirit that is as ready to leave me as water to run from a punctured water-bag! When we think thus, we are weak. Let us rather think upon the brave deeds of our ancestors! This singing spirit has a gentle voice; I am ready to follow and learn if it be an enemy or no. Let us all be found together next summer if need be!"

"Ho, ho, ho!" was the full-throated response.

"All put on your war-paint," suggested

Anookasan. "Have your knives and arrows ready!"

They did so, and all stole silently through the black forest in the direction of the mysterious sound. Clearer and clearer it came through the frosty air; but it was a foreign sound to the savage ear. Now it seemed to them almost like a distant water-fall; then it recalled the low hum of summer insects and the drowsy drone of the bumblebee. Thump, thump, thump! was the regular accompaniment.

Nearer and nearer to the cliff they came, deeper into the wild heart of the woods. At last out of the gray, formless night a dark shape appeared! It looked to them like a huge buffalo bull standing motionless in the forest, and from his throat there apparently proceeded the thump of the medicine drum, and the song of the beguiling spirit!

All of a sudden a spark went up into the air. As they continued to approach, there became visible a deep glow about the middle of the dark object. Whatever it was, they had never heard of anything like it in all their lives!

Anookasan was a little in advance of his companions, and it was he who finally discovered a wall of logs laid one upon another. Half way up there seemed to be stretched a *par-fleche* (raw-hide), from which a dim light emanated. He still thought of Oglugechana, who dwells within a hollow tree, and determined to surprise and if possible to overpower this wonder-working old man.

All now took their knives in their hands and advanced with their leader to the attack upon the log hut. " Wa-wa-wa-wa, woo, woo! " they cried. Zip, zip! went the par-fleche door and window, and they all rushed in!

There sat a man upon a roughly hewn stool. He was attired in wolfskins and wore a fox-skin cap upon his head. The larger portion of his face was clothed with natural fur. A rudely made cedar fiddle was tucked under his furred chin. Supporting it with his left hand, he sawed it vigorously with a bow that was not unlike an Indian boy's miniature weapon, while his moccasined left foot came down upon the sod floor in time with the music. When the shrill war-whoop came, and the door and window were cut in strips by the knives of the Indians, he did not even cease playing, but instinctively he closed his eyes, so as not to behold the horror of his own end.

II

IT was long ago, upon the rolling prairie south of the Devil's Lake, that a motley body of hunters gathered near a mighty herd of the bison, in the Moon of Falling Leaves. These were the first generation of the Canadian mixed-bloods, who sprang up in such numbers as to form almost a new people. These semi-wild Americans soon became a necessity to the Hudson Bay Company, as they were the greatest hunters of the bison, and made more use of this wonderful animal than even their aboriginal ancestors.

A curious race of people this, in their make-up and their customs! Their shaggy black hair was allowed to grow long, reaching to their broad shoulders, then cut off abruptly, making their heads look like a thatched house. Their dark faces were in most cases well covered with hair, their teeth large and white, and their eyes usually liquid black, although occasionally one had a tiger-brown or cold-gray eye. Their costume was a buckskin shirt with abundance of fringes, buckskin pantaloons with short leggins, a gay sash, and a cap of fox-fur. Their arms consisted of flint-lock guns, hatchets, and butcher-knives. Their ponies were small, but as hardy as themselves.

As these men gathered in the neighborhood of an immense herd of buffaloes, they busied themselves in adjusting the girths of their beautifully beaded pillow-like saddles. Among them there were exceptional riders and hunters. It was said that few could equal Antoine Michaud in feats of riding into and through the herd. There he stood, all alone, the observed of many others. It was his habit to give several Indian yells when the onset began, so as to insure a successful hunt.

In this instance, Antoine gave his usual whoops, and when they had almost reached the herd, he lifted his flint-lock over his head and plunged into the black moving mass. With a sound like the distant rumbling of thunder, those tens of thousands of buffalo hoofs were pounding the earth in retreat. Thus Antoine disappeared!

His wild steed dashed into the midst of the vast herd. Fortunately for him, the animals kept clear of him; but alas! the gap through which he had entered instantly closed again.

He yelled frantically to secure an outlet, but without effect. He had tied a red bandanna around his head to keep the hair off his face, and he now took this off and swung it crazily about him to scatter the buffalo, but it availed him nothing.

With such a mighty herd in flight, the speed could not be great; therefore the " Bois Brule " settled himself to the situation, allowing his pony to canter along slowly to save his strength. It required much tact and presence of mind to keep an open space, for the few paces of obstruction behind had gradually grown into a mile.

The mighty host moved continually southward, walking and running alternately. As the sun neared the western horizon, it fired the sky above them, and all the distant hills and prairies were in the glow of it, but immediately about them was a thick cloud of dust, and the ground appeared like a fire-swept plain.

Suddenly Antoine was aware of a tremendous push from behind. The animals smelled the cool water of a spring which formed a large bog in the midst of the plain. This solitary pond or marsh was a watering-place for the wild animals. All pushed and edged toward it; it was impossible for any one to withstand the combined strength of so many.

Antoine and his steed were in imminent danger of being pushed into the mire and trampled upon, but a mere chance brought them upon solid ground. As they were crowded across the marsh, his pony drank heartily, and he, for the first time, let go his bridle, put his two palms together for a dipper, and drank greedily of the bitter water. He had not eaten since early morning, so he now pulled up some bulrushes and ate of the tender bulbs, while the pony grazed as best he could on the tops of the tall grass.

It was now dark. The night was well-nigh intolerable for Antoine. The buffalo were about him in countless numbers, regarding him with vicious glances. It was only by reason of the natural offensiveness of man that they gave him any space. The bellowing of the bulls became general, and there was a marked uneasiness on the part of the herd. This was a sign of approaching storm, therefore the unfortunate hunter had this additional cause for anxiety. Upon the western horizon were seen some flashes of lightning.

The cloud which had been a mere speck upon the horizon had now increased to large proportions. Suddenly the wind came, and lightning flashes became more frequent, showing the ungainly forms of the animals like strange monsters in the white light. The colossal herd was again in violent motion. It was a blind rush for shelter, and no heed was paid to buffalo wallows or even deep gulches. All was in the deepest of darkness. There seemed to be groaning in heaven and earth—millions of hoofs and throats roaring in unison!

As a shipwrecked man clings to a mere fragment of wood, so Antoine, although almost exhausted with fatigue, still stuck to the back of his equally plucky pony. Death was imminent for them both. As the mad rush continued, every flash displayed heaps of bison in death struggle under the hoofs of their companions.

From time to time Antoine crossed himself and whispered a prayer to the Virgin; and again he spoke to his horse after the fashion of an Indian:

" Be brave, be strong, my horse! If we survive this trial, you shall have great honor!"

The stampede continued until they reached the bottom lands, and, like a rushing stream, their course was turned aside by the steep bank of a creek or small river. Then they moved more slowly in wide sweeps or circles, until the storm ceased, and the exhausted hunter, still in his saddle, took some snatches of sleep.

When he awoke and looked about him again it was morning. The herd had entered the strip of timber which lay on both sides of the river, and it was here that Antoine conceived his first distinct hope of saving himself.

" Waw, waw, waw! " was the hoarse cry that came to his ears, apparently from a human being in distress. Antoine strained his eyes and craned his neck to see who it could be. Through an opening in the branches ahead he perceived a large grizzly bear, lying along an inclined limb and hugging it desperately to maintain his position. The herd had now thoroughly pervaded the timber, and the bear was likewise hemmed in. He had taken to his unaccustomed refuge after making a brave stand against several bulls, one of which lay dead near by, while he himself was bleeding from many wounds.

Antoine had been assiduously looking for a friendly tree, by means of which he hoped to effect his escape from captivity by the army of bison. His horse, by chance, made his way directly under the very box-elder that was sustaining the bear and there was a convenient branch just within his reach. The Bois Brule was not then in an aggressive mood, and he saw at a glance that the occupant of the tree would not interfere with him. They were, in fact, companions in distress. Antoine tried to give a war-whoop as he sprang desperately from the pony's back and seized the cross limb with both his hands.

The hunter dangled in the air for a minute that to him seemed a year. Then he gathered up all the strength that was in him, and with one grand effort he pulled himself up on the limb.

If he had failed in this, he would have fallen to the ground under the hoofs of the buffaloes, and at their mercy.

After he had adjusted his seat as comfortably as he could, Antoine surveyed the situation. He had at least escaped from sudden and certain death. It grieved him that he had been forced to abandon his horse, and he had no idea how far he had come nor any means of returning to his friends, who had, no doubt, given him up for lost. His immediate needs were rest and food.

Accordingly he selected a fat cow and emptied into her sides one barrel of his gun, which had been slung across his chest. He went on shooting until he had killed many fat cows, greatly to the discomfiture of his neighbor, the bear, while the bison vainly struggled among themselves to keep the fatal spot clear.

By the middle of the afternoon the main body of the herd had passed, and Antoine was sure that his captivity had at last come to an end. Then he swung himself from his limb to the ground, and walked stiffly to the carcass of the nearest cow, which he dressed and prepared himself a meal. But first he took a piece of liver on a long pole to the bear!

Antoine finally decided to settle in the recesses of the heavy timber for the winter, as he was on foot and alone, and not able to travel any great distance. He jerked the meat of all the animals he had killed, and prepared their skins for bedding and clothing. The Bois Brule and Ami, as he called the bear, soon became necessary to one another. The former considered the bear very good company, and the latter had learned that man's business, after all, is not to kill every animal he meets. He had been fed and kindly treated, when helpless from his wounds, and this he could not forget.

Antoine was soon busy erecting a small log hut, while the other partner kept a sharp lookout, and, after his hurts were healed, often brought in some small game. The two had a perfect understanding without many words; at least, the speech was all upon one side! In his leisure moments Antoine had occupied himself with whittling out a rude fiddle of cedar-wood, strung with the guts of a wild cat that he had killed. Every evening that winter he would sit down after supper and play all the old familiar pieces, varied with improvisations of his own. At first, the music and the incessant pounding time with his foot annoyed the bear. At times, too, the Canadian would call out the figures for the dance. All this Ami became accustomed to in time, and even showed no small interest in the buzzing of the little cedar box. Not infrequently, he was out in the evening, and the human partner was left alone. It chanced, quite fortunately, that the bear was absent on the night that the red folk rudely invaded the lonely hut.

The calmness of the strange being had stayed their hands. They had never before seen a man of other race than their own!

" Is this Chanotedah? Is he man, or beast? " the warriors asked one another.

" Ho, wake up, koda! " exclaimed Anooka-san. " Maybe he is of the porcupine tribe, ashamed to look at us! "

At this moment they spied the haunch of venison which swung from a cross-stick over a fine bed of coals, in front of the rude mud chimney.

" Ho, koda has something to eat! Sit down, sit down! " they shouted to one another.

Now Antoine opened his eyes for the first time upon his unlooked-for guests. They were a haggard and hungry-looking set. Anookasan extended his hand, and Antoine gave it a hearty shake. He set his fiddle against the wall and began to cut up the smoking venison into generous pieces and place it before them. All ate like famished men, while the firelight intensified the red paint upon their wild and warlike faces.

When he had satisfied his first hunger, Anookasan spoke in signs. "Friend, we have never before heard a song like that of your little cedar box! We had supposed it to be a spirit, or some harmful thing, hence our attack upon it. We never saw any people of your sort. What is your tribe?"

Antoine explained his plight in the same manner, and the two soon came to an understanding. The Canadian told the starving hunters of a buffalo herd a little way to the north, and one of their number was dispatched homeward with the news. In two days the entire band reached Antoine's place. The Bois Brule was treated with kindness and honor, and the tribe gave him a wife. Suffice it to say that Antoine lived and died among the Yanktons at a good old age; but Ami could not brook the invasion upon their hermit life. He was never seen after that first evening.

IV

THE FAMINE

ON the Assiniboine River in western Manitoba there stands an old, historic trading-post, whose crumbling walls crown a high promontory in the angle formed by its junction with a tributary stream. This is Fort Ellis, a mistress of the wilderness and lodestone of savage tribes between the years 1830 and 1870.

Hither at that early day the Indians brought their buffalo robes and beaver skins to exchange for merchandise, ammunition, and the "spirit water." Among the others there presently appeared a band of renegade Sioux—the exiles, as they called themselves—under White Lodge, whose father, Little Crow, had been a leader in the outbreak of 1862. Now the great war-chief was dead, and his people were prisoners or fugitives. The shrewd Scotch trader, McLeod, soon discovered that the Sioux were

[100]

skilled hunters, and therefore he exerted himself to befriend them, as well as to encourage a
feeling of good will between them and the Canadian tribes who were accustomed to make the
old fort their summer rendezvous.

Now the autumn had come, after a long summer of feasts and dances, and the three tribes
broke up and dispersed as usual in various directions.   White Lodge had twin daughters,
very handsome, whose ears had been kept burning with the proposals of many suitors, but none
had received any definite encouragement.   There
were one or two who would have been quite
willing to forsake their own tribes and follow
the exiles had they not feared too much the
ridicule of the braves.   Even Angus McLeod,
the trader's eldest son, had need of all his
patience and caution, for he had never seen
any woman he admired so much as the piquant
Magaskawee, called The Swan, one of these
belles of the forest.

The Sioux journeyed northward, toward the
Mouse River. They had wintered on that
stream before, and it was then the feeding

ground of large herds of buffalo. When it was discovered that the herds were moving westward, across the Missouri, there was no little apprehension. The shrewd medicine-man became aware of the situation, and hastened to announce his prophecy:

" The Great Mystery has appeared to me in a dream! He showed me men with haggard and thin faces. I interpret this to mean a scarcity of food during the winter."

The chief called his counselors together and set before them the dream of the priest, whose prophecy, he said, was already being fulfilled in part by the westward movement of the buffalo. It was agreed that they should lay up all the dried meat they could obtain; but even for this they were too late. The storms were already at hand, and that winter was more severe than any that the old men could recall in their traditions. The braves killed all the small game for a wide circuit around the camp, but the buffalo had now crossed the river, and that country was not favorable for deer. The more enterprising young men organized hunting expeditions to various parts of the open prairie, but each time they returned with empty hands.

The "Moon of Sore Eyes," or March, had come at last, and Wazeah, the God of Storm, was still angry. Their scant provision of dried meat had held out wonderfully, but it was now all but consumed. The Sioux had but little ammunition, and the snow was still so deep that it was impossible for them to move away to any other region in search of game. The worst was feared; indeed, some of the children and feeble old people had already succumbed.

White Lodge again called his men together in council, and it was determined to send a messenger to Fort Ellis to ask for relief. A young man called Face-the-Wind was chosen for his exceptional qualities of speed and endurance upon long journeys. The old medicine-man, whose shrewd prophecy had gained for him the confidence of the people, now came forward. He had closely observed the appearance of the messenger selected, and had taken note of the storm and distance. Accordingly he said:

"My children, the Great Mystery is offended, and this is the cause of all our suffering! I see a shadow hanging over our messenger, but I will pray to the Great Spirit—perhaps he may yet save him!—Great Mystery, be thou merciful! Strengthen this young man for his journey, that he may be able to finish it and to send us aid! If we see the sun of summer again, we will offer the choicest of our meats to thee, and do thee great honor!"

During this invocation, as occasionally happens in March, a loud peal of thunder was heard. This coincidence threw the prophet almost into a frenzy, and the poor people were all of a tremble. Face-the-Wind believed that the prayer was directly answered, and though weakened by fasting and unfit for the task before him, he was encouraged to make the attempt.

He set out on the following day at dawn, and on the third day staggered into the fort, looking like a specter and almost frightening the people. He was taken to McLeod's house and given good care. The poor fellow, delirious with hunger, fancied himself engaged in mortal combat with Eyah, the god of famine, who has a mouth extending from ear to ear. Wherever he goes there is famine, for he swallows all that he sees, even whole nations!

The legend has it that Eyah fears nothing but the jingling of metal: so finally the dying man looked up into McLeod's face and cried: " Ring your bell in his face, Wahadah! "

The kind-hearted factor could not refuse, and as the great bell used to mark the hours of work and of meals pealed out untimely upon the frosty air, the Indian started up and in that moment breathed his last. He had given no news, and McLeod and his sons could only guess at the state of affairs upon the Mouse River.

While the men were in council with her father, Magaskawee had turned over the contents of her work-bag. She had found a small roll of birch-bark in which she kept her porcupine quills for embroidery, and pulled the delicate layers apart. The White Swan was not altogether the untutored Indian maiden, for she had lived in the family of a missionary in the States, and had learned both to speak and write some English. There was no ink, no pen or pencil, but with her bone awl she pressed upon the white side of the bark the following words :

MR. ANGUS McLEOD:—

We are near the hollow rock on the Mouse River. The buffalo went away across the Missouri, and our powder and shot are gone. We are starving. Good-bye, if I don't see you again.

MAGASKAWEE.

The girl entrusted this little note to her grandmother, and she in turn gave it to the messenger. But he, as we know, was unable to deliver it.

" Angus, tell the boys to bury the poor fellow to-morrow. I dare say he brought us some news from White Lodge, but we have got to go to the happy hunting-grounds to get it, or wait till the exile band returns in the spring. Evidently," continued McLeod, " he fell sick on the way: or else he was starving ! "

This last suggestion horrified Angus. " I believe, father," he exclaimed, " that we ought to examine his bundle."

A small oblong packet was brought forth from the dead man's belt and carefully unrolled.

There were several pairs of moccasins, and within one of these Angus found something wrapped up nicely. He proceeded to unwind the long strings of deerskin with which it was securely tied, and brought forth a thin sheet of birch-bark. At first, there seemed to be nothing more, but a closer scrutiny revealed the impression of the awl, and the bit of nature's parchment was brought nearer to his face, and scanned with a zeal equal to that of any student of ancient hieroglyphics.

"This tells the whole story, father!" exclaimed the young man at last. "Magaska-wee's note—just listen!" and he read it aloud. "I shall start to-morrow. We can take enough provision and ammunition on two sleds, with six dogs to each. I shall want three good men to go with me." Angus spoke with decision.

"Well, we can't afford to lose our best hunters; and you might also bring home with you

what furs and robes they have on hand," was
his father's prudent reply.

"I don't care particularly for the skins,"
Angus declared; but he at once began hurried
preparations for departure.

In the meantime affairs grew daily more
desperate in the exile village on the far-away
Mouse River, and a sort of Indian hopelessness
and resignation settled down upon the little
community. There were few who really expected their messenger to reach the fort, or believed that even if he did so, relief would be
sent in time to save them. White Lodge, the
father of his people, was determined to share
with them the last mouthful of food, and every
morning Winona and Magaskawee went with
scanty portions in their hands to those whose
supply had entirely failed.

On the outskirts of the camp there dwelt an
old woman with an orphan grandchild, who
had been denying herself for some time in order
that the child might live longer. This poor
teepee the girls visited often, and one on each
side they raised the exhausted woman and

poured into her mouth the warm broth they had brought with them.

It was on the very day Face-the-Wind reached Fort Ellis that a young hunter who had ventured further from the camp than any one else had the luck to bring down a solitary deer with his bow and arrow. In his weakness he had reached camp very late, bearing the deer with the utmost difficulty upon his shoulders. It was instantly separated into as many pieces as there were lodges of the famishing Sioux. These delicious morsels were hastily cooked and eagerly devoured, but among so many there was scarcely more than a mouthful to the share of each, and the brave youth himself did not receive enough to appease in the least his craving!

On the eve of Angus' departure for the exile village, Three Stars, a devoted suitor of Winona's, accompanied by another Assiniboine brave, appeared unexpectedly at the fort. He at once asked permission to join the relief party, and they set out at daybreak.

The lead-dog was the old reliable Mack, who

had been in service for several seasons on winter trips. All of the white men were clad in
buckskin shirts and pantaloons, with long
fringes down the sides, fur caps and fur-lined
moccasins. Their guns were fastened to the
long, toboggan-like sleds.

The snow had thawed a little and formed an
icy crust, and over this fresh snow had fallen,
which a northwest wind swept over the surface
like ashes after a prairie fire. The sun appeared
for a little time in the morning, but it seemed
as if he were cutting short his course on account
of the bleak day, and had protected himself
with pale rings of fire.

The dogs laid back their ears, drew in their
tails, and struck into their customary trot, but
even old Mack looked back frequently, as if
reluctant to face such a pricking and scarifying
wind. The men felt the cold still more keenly,
although they had taken care to cover every bit
of the face except one eye, and that was completely blinded at times by the granulated snow.

The sun early retreated behind a wall of cloud,
and the wind moaned and wailed like a living

creature in anguish. At last they approached the creek where they had planned to camp for the night. There was nothing to be seen but a few stunted willows half buried in the drifts, but the banks of the little stream afforded some protection from the wind.

" Whoa ! " shouted the leader, and the dogs all stopped, sitting down on their haunches. " Come, Mack ! " (with a wave of the hand), " lead your fellows down to the creek ! "

The old dog started down at the word, and all the rest followed. A space was quickly cleared of snow, while one man scoured the thickets in search of brush for fuel. In a few minutes the tent was up and a fire kindled in the center, while the floor was thickly strewn with twigs of willow, over which buffalo robes were spread. Three Stars attended to supper, and soon in the midst of the snapping willow fire a kettle was boiling. All partook of strong tea, dried meat of buffalo, and pemmican, a mixture of pounded dried meat with wild cherries and melted fat. The dogs, to whom one-half the tent was assigned, enjoyed a hearty meal and fell into a deep sleep, lying one against another.

After supper Jerry drove two sticks into the ground, one on each side of the fire, and connected the two by a third one over the blaze. Upon this all hung their socks to dry—most of them merely square pieces of blanket cut to serve that purpose. Soon each man rolled himself in his own buffalo robe and fell asleep.

All night the wind raged. The lonely teepee now and then shuddered violently, as a stronger blast than usual almost lifted it from the ground. No one stirred except from time to time one of the dogs, who got up snarling and sniffing the cold air, turned himself round several times as if on a pivot, and finally lay down for another nap.

In the morning the travelers one by one raised their heads and looked through the smoke-hole, then fell back again with a grunt. All the world appeared without form and void. Presently, however, the light of the sun was seen as if through a painted window, and by afternoon they were able to go on, the wind having partially subsided. This was only a taste of the weather encountered by the party on their unseasonable trip; but had it been ten times harder, it would never have occurred to Angus to turn back.

On the third day the rescuers approached the camp of the exiles. There was an ominous quiet; no creature was to be seen; but the smoke which ascended into the air in perpendicular columns assured them that some, at least, were still alive. The party happened to reach first the teepee of the poor old woman who had been so faithfully ministered to by the twin sisters. They had no longer any food to give, but they had come to build her fire, if she should have survived the night. At the very door of the lodge they heard the jingle of dog-bells, but they had not time to announce the joyful news before the men were in sight.

In another minute Angus and Three Stars were beside them, holding their wasted hands.

V

THE CHIEF SOLDIER

JUST outside of a fine large wigwam of smoke-tanned buffalo-skins stood Tawasuota, very early upon an August morning of the year 1862. Behind the wigwam there might have been seen a thrifty patch of growing maize, whose tall, graceful stalks resembled as many warriors in dancing-dresses and tasseled head-gear.

"Thanks be to the 'Great Mystery,' I have been successful in the fortunes of war! None can say that Tawasuota is a coward. I have done well; so well that our chief, Little Crow, has offered me the honored position of his chief soldier, ta ákich-ítah!" he said to himself with satisfaction.

The sun was just over the eastern bank of the Minnesota River, and he could distinctly see upon the level prairie the dwellings of logs which had sprung up there during the year, since Little Crow's last treaty with the whites. "Ugh! they are taking from us our beautiful and game-teeming country!" was his thought as he gazed upon them.

At that moment, out of the conical white teepee, in shape like a new-born mushroom, there burst two little frisky boys, leaping and whooping. They were clad gracefully in garments of fine deerskin, and each wore a miniature feather upon his head, marking them as children of a distinguished warrior.

They danced nimbly around their father, while he stood with all the dignity of a buck elk, viewing the landscape reddened by sunrise and the dwellers therein, the old and the new, the red and the white. He noticed that they were still unmingled; the river divided them.

At last he took the dancing little embryo warriors one in either hand, and lifted them to his majestic shoulders. There he placed them in perfect poise. His haughty spirit found a moment's happiness in fatherhood.

Suddenly Tawasuota set the two boys on the ground again, and signed to them to enter the teepee. Apparently all was quiet. The camps and villages of the Minnesota reservation were undisturbed, so far as he could see, save by the awakening of nature; and the early risers among his people moved about in seeming security, while the smoke of their morning fires arose one by one into the blue. Still the warrior gazed steadily westward, up the river, whence his quick ear had caught the faint but ominous sound of a distant war-whoop.

The ridge beyond the Wahpeton village bounded the view, and between this point and his own village were the agency buildings and the traders' stores. The Indian's keen eye swept the horizon, and finally alighted once more upon the home of his new neighbor across the river, the flaxen-haired white man with many children, who with his white squaw and his little ones worked from sunrise to sunset, much like the beaver family.

Ah! the distant war-whoop once more saluted his ear, but this time nearer and more distinct.

"What! the Rice Creek band is coming in full war-paint! Can it be another Ojibway attack? Ugh, ugh! I will show their warriors again this day what it is to fight!" he exclaimed aloud.

The white traders and Government employees, those of them who were up and about, heard and saw the advancing column of warriors. Yet they showed no sign of anxiety or fear. Most of them thought that there might be some report of Ojibways coming to attack the Sioux,—a not uncommon incident,—and that those warriors were on their way to the post to replenish their powder-horns. A few of the younger men were delighted with the prospect of witnessing an Indian fight.

On swept the armed band, in numbers increasing at every village.

It was true that there had been a growing feeling of distrust among the Indians, because their annuities had been withheld for a long time, and the money payments had been delayed again and again. There were many in great need. The traders had given them credit to some extent (charging them four times the value of the article purchased), and had likewise induced Little Crow to sign over to them ninety-eight thousand dollars, the purchase-price of that part of their reservation lying north of the Minnesota, and already occupied by the whites.

This act had made the chief very unpopular, and he was ready for a desperate venture to regain his influence. Certain warriors among the upper bands of Sioux had even threatened his life, but no one spoke openly of a break with the whites.

When, therefore, the news came to Little Crow that some roving hunters of the Rice Creek band had killed in a brawl two families of white settlers, he saw his opportunity to show once for all to the disaffected that he had no love for the white man. Immediately he sprang upon his white horse, and prepared to make their cause a general one among his people.

Tawasuota had scarcely finished his hasty preparations for war, by painting his face and seeing to the loading of his gun, when he heard the voice of Little Crow outside his lodge.

" You are now my head soldier," said the

[118]

chief, "and this is your first duty. Little Six and his band have inaugurated the war against the whites. They have already wiped out two families, and are now on their way to the agency. Let my chief soldier fire the first shot.

"Those Indians who have cut their hair and donned the white man's clothing may give the warning; so make haste! If you fall to-day, there is no better day on which to die, and the women of our tribe will weep proud tears for Tawasuota. I leave it with you to lead my warriors." With these words the wily chief galloped away to meet the war-party.

"Here comes Little Crow, the friend of the white man!" exclaimed a warrior, as he approached.

"Friends and warriors, you will learn to-day who are the friends of the white man, and none will dare again to insinuate that I have been against the interests of my own people," he replied.

After a brief consultation with the chiefs he advised the traders:

"Do not hesitate to fill the powder-horns of

[119]

my warriors; they may be compelled to fight all day."

Soon loud yells were heard along the road to the Indian village.

" Ho, ho! Tawasuota u ye do! " (" He is coming ; he is coming! ") shouted the warriors in chorus.

The famous war-chief dismounted in silence, gun in hand, and walked directly toward the larger store.

" Friend," he exclaimed, " we may both meet the ' Great Mystery ' to-day, but you must go first."

There was a loud report, and the unsuspecting white man lay dead. It was James Lynd, one of the early traders, and a good friend to the Indians.

No sooner had Tawasuota fired the fatal shot than every other Indian discharged his piece. Hither and thither ran the frantic people, seeking safety, but seeking it in vain. They were wholly unprepared and at the mercy of the foe.

The friendly Indians, too, were taken entirely by surprise. They had often heard wild talk of revolt, but it had never had the indorsement of intelligent chiefs, or of such a number as to carry any weight to their minds. Christian Indians rushed in every direction to save, if possible, at least the wives and children of the Government employees. Meanwhile, the new white settlements along the Minnesota River were utterly unconscious of any danger. Not a soul dreamed of the terrible calamity that each passing moment was bringing nearer and nearer.

Tawasuota stepped aside, and took up his pipe. He seemed almost oblivious of what he had done. While the massacre still raged about him in all its awful cruelty, he sat smoking and trying to think collectedly, but his mind was confused, and in his secret thoughts he rebelled against Little Crow. It was a cowardly deed that he had been ordered to commit, he thought; for he had won his reputation solely by brave deeds in battle, and this was more like murdering one of his own tribesmen—this killing of an unarmed white man. Up to this time the killing of a white man was not counted the deed of a warrior; it was murder.

The lesser braves might now satisfy their spite against the traders to their hearts' content, but Tawasuota had been upon the best of terms with all of them.

Suddenly a ringing shout was heard. The chief soldier looked up, and beheld a white man, nearly nude, leap from the roof of the larger store and alight upon the ground hard by him.

He had emptied one barrel of his gun, and, if he chose to do so, could have killed Myrick then and there; but he made no move, exclaiming:

"Ho, ho! Nina iyaye!" ("Run, run!")

Away sped the white man in the direction of the woods and the river.

"Ah, he is swift; he will save himself," thought Tawasuota.

All the Indians had now spied the fugitive; they yelled and fired at him again and again, as if they were shooting at a running deer; but he only ran faster. Just as he had reached the very edge of the sheltering timber a single shot rang out, and he fell headlong.

A loud war-whoop went up, for many believed that this was one of the men who had stolen their trust funds.

Tawasuota continued to sit and smoke in the shade while the carnage and plunder that he had set on foot proceeded on all sides of him. Presently men began to form small parties to cross the river on their mission of death, but he refused to join any of them. At last, several of the older warriors came up to smoke with him.

"Ho, nephew," said one of them with much gravity, "you have precipitated a dreadful calamity. This means the loss of our country, the destruction of our nation. What were you thinking of?"

It was the Wahpeton chief who spoke, a blood-relation to Tawasuota. He did not at once reply, but filled his pipe in silence, and handed it to the man who thus reproached him. It was a just rebuke; for he was a brave man, and he could have refused the request of his chief to open the massacre.

At this moment it was announced that a body

of white soldiers were on the march from Fort Ridgeley. A large body of warriors set out to meet them.

"Nephew, you have spilled the first blood of the white man; go, join in battle with the soldiers. They are armed; they can defend themselves," remarked the old chief, and Tawasuota replied:

"Uncle, you speak truth; I have committed the act of a coward. It was not of my own will I did it; nevertheless, I have raised my weapon, and I will fight the whites as long as I live. If I am ever taken, they will first have to kill me." He arose, took up his gun, and joined the war-party.

The dreadful day of massacre was almost ended. The terrified Sioux women and children had fled up the river before the approaching troops. Long shafts of light from the setting sun painted every hill; one side red as with blood, the other dark as the shadow of death. A cloud of smoke from burning homes hung over the beautiful river. Even the permanent dwellings of the Indians were empty, and all the teepees which had dotted with their white cones the west bank of the Minnesota had disappeared. Here and there were small groups of warriors returning from their bloody work, and among them was Tawasuota.

He looked long at the spot where his home had stood; but it was gone, and with it his family. Ah, the beautiful country of his ancestors! he must depart from it forever, for he knew now that the white man would occupy that land. Sadly he sang the spirit-song, and made his appeal to the "Great Mystery," excusing himself by the plea that what he had done had been in the path of duty. There was no glory in it for him; he could wear no eagle feather, nor could he ever recount the deed. It was dreadful to him—the thought that he had fired upon an unarmed and helpless man.

The chief soldier followed the broad trail of the fleeing host, and after some hours he came upon a camp. There were no war-songs nor dances there, as was their wont after a battle, but a strange stillness reigned. Even the dogs scarcely barked at his approach; everything seemed conscious of the awful carnage of the day.

He stopped at a tent and inquired after his beautiful wife and two little sons, whom he had already trained to uphold their father's reputation, but was directed to his mother's teepee.

"Ah, my son, my son, what have you done?" cried his old mother when she saw him. "Come in, come in; let us eat together once more ; for I have a foreboding that it is for the last time. Alas, what have you done?"

Tawasuota silently entered the tent of his widowed mother, and his three sisters gave him the place of honor.

"Mother, it is not right to blame our brother," said the eldest. "He was the chief's head soldier; and if he had disobeyed his orders, he would have been called a coward. That he could not bear."

Food was handed him, and he swallowed a few mouthfuls, and gave back the dish.

"You have not yet told me where she is, and the children," he said with a deep sigh.

"My son, my son, I have not, because it will

give you pain. I wanted you to eat first! She has been taken away by her own mother to Faribault, among the white people. I could not persuade them to wait until you came. Her people are lovers of the whites. They have even accepted their religion," grieved the good old mother.

Tawasuota's head dropped upon his chest, and he sat silent for a long time. The mother and three sisters were also silent, for they knew how heavy his grief must be. At last he spoke.

" Mother, I am too proud to desert the tribe now and join my wife among the white people. My brother-in-law may lie in my behalf, and say that my hands are not stained with blood; but the spirits of those who died to-day would rebuke me, and the rebuke would be just. No, I must fight the whites until I die; and neither have I fought without cause; but I must see my sons once more before I go."

When Tawasuota left his mother's teepee he walked fast across the circle toward the council lodge to see Little Crow. He drew his blanket closely about him, with his gun underneath. The keen eye of the wily chief detected the severe expression upon the face of his guest, and he hastened to speak first.

" There are times in the life of every great man when he must face hardship and put self aside for the good of his people. You have done well to-day! "

" I care little for myself," replied Tawasu-ota, " but my heart is heavy to-night. My wife and two boys have been taken away among the whites by my mother-in-law. I fear for their safety, when it is known what we have done."

" Ugh, that old woman is too hasty in accepting the ways of the stranger people! " exclaimed the chief.

" I am now on my way to see them," declared Tawasuota.

" Ugh, ugh, I shall need you to-morrow! My plan is to attack the soldiers at Fort Ridgeley with a strong force. There are not many. Then we shall attack New Ulm and other towns. We will drive them all back into Saint Paul and Fort Snelling." Little Crow spoke with energy.

" You must stay," he added, " and lead the attack either at the fort or at New Ulm."

For some minutes the chief soldier sat in silence.

At last he said simply, " I will do it."

On the following day the attack was made, but it was unsuccessful. The whole State was now alarmed, and all the frontier settlers left alive had flocked to the larger and more protected towns. It had also developed during the day that there was a large party of Sioux who were ready to surrender, thereby showing that they had not been party to the massacre nor indorsed the hasty action of the tribe.

At evening Tawasuota saw that there would be a long war with the whites, and that the Indians must remove their families out of danger. The feeling against all Indians was great. Night had brought him no relief of mind, but it promised to shield him in a hazardous undertaking. He consulted no one, but set out for the distant village of Faribault.

He kept to the flats back of the Minnesota, away from the well-traveled roads, and moved

on at a good gait, for he realized that he had
to cover a hundred miles in as few hours as
possible. Every day that passed would make
it more difficult for him to rejoin his family.

Although he kept as far as he could from the
settlements, he would come now and then upon
a solitary frame house, razed to the ground by
the war-parties of the day before. The members of the ill-fated family were to be seen scattered in and about the place; and their white,
upturned faces told him that his race must pay
for the deed.

The dog that howled pitifully over the dead
was often the only survivor of the farmer's
household.

Occasionally Tawasuota heard at a distance
the wagons of the fugitives, loaded with women
and children, while armed men walked before
and behind. These caravans were usually
drawn by oxen and moved slowly toward some
large town.

When the dawn appeared in the east, the
chief soldier was compelled to conceal himself
in a secluded place. He rolled up in his

blanket, lay down in a dry creek-bed among the red willows and immediately fell asleep.

With the next evening he resumed his journey, and reached Faribault toward midnight. Even here every approach was guarded against the possibility of an Indian attack. But there was much forest, and he knew the country well. He reconnoitred, and soon found the Indian community, but dared not approach and enter, for these Indians had allied themselves with the whites; they would be charged with treachery if it were known that they had received a hostile Sioux, and none were so hated by the white people as Little Crow and his war-chief.

He chose a concealed position from which he might watch the movements of his wife, if she were indeed there, and had not been waylaid and slain on the journey hither.

That night was the hardest one that the warrior had ever known. If he slept, it was only to dream of the war-whoop and attack; but at last he found himself broad awake, the sun well up, and yes! there were his two little sons, playing outside their teepee as of old. The next moment he heard the voice of his wife from the deep woods wailing for her husband!

"Oh, take us, husband, take us with you! let us all die together!" she pleaded as she clung to him whom she had regarded as already dead; for she knew of the price that had been put upon his head, and that some of the half-breeds loved money better than the blood of their Indian mothers.

Tawasuota stood for a minute without speaking, while his huge frame trembled like a mighty pine beneath the thunderbolt.

"No," he said at last. "I shall go, but you must remain. You are a woman, and the white people need not know that your little boys are mine. Bring them here to me this evening that I may kiss them farewell."

The sun was hovering among the treetops when they met again.

"Atay! atay!" ("Papa, papa!") the little fellows cried out in spite of her cautions; but the mother put her finger to her lips, and they became silent. Tawasuota took each boy in his arms, and held him close for a few moments;

he smiled to them, but large tears rolled down his cheeks. Then he disappeared in the shadows, and they never saw him again.

The chief soldier lived and died a warrior and an enemy to the white man; but one of his two sons became in after-years a minister of the Christian gospel, under the "Long-Haired Praying Man," Bishop Whipple, of Minnesota.

VI

THE WHITE MAN'S ERRAND

UPON the wide tableland that lies at the back of a certain Indian agency, a camp of a thousand teepees was pitched in a circle, according to the ancient usage. In the center of the circle stood the council lodge, where there were gathered together of an afternoon all the men of years and distinction, some in blankets, some in uniform, and still others clad in beggarly white man's clothing. But the minds of all were alike upon the days of their youth and freedom.

Around the council fire they passed and repassed the pipe of peace, and when the big drum was struck they sang the accompaniment with sad yet pleasant thoughts of the life that is past. Between the songs stories of brave deeds and dangerous exploits were related by the actors in turn, with as much spirit and zest as if they were still living in those days.

"Tum, tum, tum," the drum was sounded.

" Oow, oow! " they hooted in a joyous chorus at the close of each refrain.

" Ho! " exclaimed finally the master of ceremonies for the evening. " It is Zuyamani's story of his great ride that we should now hear! It was not far from this place, upon the Missouri River, and within the recollection of many of us that this occurred. Ye young men must hear! "

" Ho, ho! " was the ready response of all present, and the drum was struck once according to custom. The pipe was filled and handed to Zuyamani, who gravely smoked for a few moments in silence. Then he related his contribution to the unwritten history of our frontier in these words :

" It was during the winter following that summer in which General Sibley pursued many of our people across the Muddy River (1863), that we Hunkpatees, friendly Sioux, were camping at a place called ' Hunt-the-Deer,' about two miles from Fort Rice, Dakota Territory.

" The Chief Soldier of the garrison called one day upon the leading chiefs of our band. To each one he said: 'Lend me your bravest warrior!' Each chief called his principal warriors together and laid the matter before them.

" 'The Chief Soldier at this place,' they explained, 'wants to send a message to Fort Berthold, where the Rees and Mandans live, to another Chief Soldier there. The soldiers of the Great Father do not know the way, neither could any of them get through the lines. He asks for a brave man to carry his message.'

" The Mandans and the Rees were our hereditary enemies, but this was not the principal reason for our hesitation. We had declared allegiance to the Great Father at Washington; we had taken our stand against the fighting men of our own nation, and the hostile Sioux were worse than enemies to us at this time!

" Each chief had only called on his leading warriors, and each in turn reported his failure to secure a volunteer.

" Then the Chief Soldier sent again and said: 'Is there not a young man among you who dares to face death? If he reaches the fort with my message, he will need to be quick-witted as well as brave, and the Great Father will not forget him!'

"Now all the chiefs together called all the young men in a great council, and submitted to them the demand of the Great Father's servant. We knew well that the country between us and Fort Berthold, about one hundred and fifty miles distant, was alive with hostile Sioux, and that if any of us should be caught and recognized by them, he would surely be put to death. It would not be easy to deceive them by professing hostility to the Government, for the record of each individual Indian is well known. The warriors were still unwilling to go, for they argued thus: 'This is a white man's errand, and will not be recorded as a brave deed upon the honor roll of our people.' I think many would have volunteered but for that belief. At that time we had not a high opinion of the white man.

"Since all the rest were silent, it came into my mind to offer my services. The warriors looked at me in astonishment, for I was a very young man and had no experience.

"Our chief, Two Bears, who was my own

uncle, finally presented my name to the commanding officer. He praised my courage and begged me to be vigilant. The interpreter told him that I had never been upon the war-path and would be knocked over like a rabbit, but as no one else would go, he was obliged to accept me as his messenger. He gave me a fine horse and saddle; also a rifle and soldier's uniform. I would not take the gun nor wear the blue coat. I accepted only a revolver, and I took my bow and quiver full of arrows, and wore my usual dress. I hid the letter in my moccasin.

" I set out before daybreak the next morning. The snow was deep. I rode up the river, on the west bank, keeping a very close watch all the way, but seeing nothing. I had been provided with a pair of field glasses, and I surveyed the country on all sides from the top of every hill. Having traveled all day and part of the night, I rested my horse and I took a little sleep.

" After eating a small quantity of pemmican, I made a very early start in the morning. It was scarcely light when I headed for a near-by ridge from which to survey the country beyond. Just

as I ascended the rise I found myself almost surrounded by loose ponies, evidently belonging to
a winter camp of the hostile Sioux.

" I readjusted my saddle, tightened the girths,
and prepared to ride swiftly around the camp.
I saw some men already out after ponies. No
one appeared to have seen me as yet, but I felt
that as soon as it became lighter they could not
help observing me. I turned to make the circuit
of the camp, which was a very large one, and
as soon as I reached the timbered bottom lands
I began to congratulate myself that I had not
been seen.

" As I entered the woods at the crossing of a
dry creek, I noticed that my horse was nervous.
I knew that horses are quick to discover animals
or men by scent, and I became nervous, too.

" The animal put his four feet together and
almost slid down the steep bank. As he came
out on the opposite side he swerved suddenly and
started to run. Then I saw a man watching me
from behind a tree. Fortunately for me, he
carried no weapon. He was out after ponies,
and had only a lariat wound upon one shoulder.

" He beckoned and made signs for me to stop, but I spurred my horse and took flight at once. I could hear him yelling far behind me, no doubt to arouse the camp and set them on my trail.

" As I fled westward, I came upon another man, mounted, and driving his ponies before him. He yelled and hooted in vain; then turned and rode after me. Two others had started in pursuit, but my horse was a good one, and I easily outdistanced them at the start.

" After I had fairly circled the camp, I turned again toward the river, hoping to regain the bottom lands. The traveling was bad. Sometimes we came to deep gulches filled with snow, where my horse would sink in up to his body and seem unable to move. When I jumped off his back and struck him once or twice, he would make several desperate leaps and recover his footing. My pursuers were equally hindered, but by this time the pursuit was general, and in order to terrify me they yelled continually and fired their guns into the air. Now and then I came to a gulch which I had to follow up in search of a place to cross, and at such times they gained on me. I began to despair, for I knew that the white man's horses have not the endurance of our Indian ponies, and I expected to be chased most of the day.

" Finally I came to a ravine that seemed impossible to cross. As I followed it up, it became evident that some of them had known of this trap, and had cut in ahead of me. I felt that I must soon abandon my horse and slide down the steep sides of the gulch to save myself.

" However, I made one last effort to pass my enemies. They came within gunshot and several fired at me, although all our horses were going at full speed. They missed me, and being at last clear of them, I came to a place where I could cross, and the pursuit stopped."

When Zuyamani reached this point in his recital, the great drum was struck several times, and all the men cheered him.

" The days are short in winter," he went on after a short pause, " and just now the sun sank behind the hills. I did not linger. I continued my journey by night, and reached Fort Berthold before midnight. I had been so thoroughly frightened and was so much exhausted that I did not want to talk, and as soon as I had delivered my letters to the post commander, I went to the interpreter's quarters to sleep.

"The interpreter, however, announced my arrival, and that same night many Ree, Gros Ventre, and Mandan warriors came to call upon me. Among them was a great chief of the Rees, called Poor Dog.

"'You must be,' said he to me, 'either a very young man, or a fool! You have not told us about your close escape, but a runner came in at dusk and told us of the pursuit. He reported that you had been killed by the hostiles, for he heard many guns fired about the middle of the afternoon. These white men will never give you any credit for your wonderful ride, nor will they compensate you for the risks you have taken in their service. They will not give you so much as one eagle feather for what you have done!'

"The next day I was sent for to go to headquarters, and there I related my all-day pursuit by the hostile Sioux. The commanding officer

advised me to remain at the fort fifteen days
before making the return trip, thinking that by
that time my enemies might cease to look for me.

"At the end of the fortnight he wrote his
letters, and I told him that I was ready to start.
'I will give you,' he said, 'twenty Rees and
Gros Ventres to escort you past the hostile
camp.' We set out very early and rode all day,
so that night overtook us just before we reached
the camp.

"At nightfall we sent two scouts ahead, but
before they left us they took the oath of the
pipe in token of their loyalty. You all know the
ancient war custom. A lighted pipe was held
toward them and each one solemnly touched it,
after which it was passed as usual.

"We followed more slowly, and at about
midnight we came to the place where our scouts
had agreed to meet us. They were to return
from a reconnaissance of the camp and report
on what they had seen. It was a lonely spot,
and the night was very cold and still. We sat
there in the snowy woods near a little creek and
smoked in silence while we waited. I had plenty

of time to reflect upon my position. These
Gros Ventres and Rees have been our enemies
for generations. I was one man to twenty!
They had their orders from the commander of
the fort, and that was my only safeguard.

" Soon we heard the howl of a wolf a little
to the westward. Immediately one of the party
answered in the same manner. I could not have
told it from the howl of a real wolf. Then we
heard a hooting owl down the creek. Another
of our party hooted like an owl.

" Presently the wolf's voice sounded nearer,
while the owl's hoot came nearer in the opposite
direction. Then we heard the footsteps of
ponies on the crisp, frosty air. The scout who
had been imitating the wolf came in first, and
the owl soon followed. The warriors made a
ring and again filled the pipe, and the scouts
took the oath for the second time.

" After smoking, they reported a trail going
up a stream tributary to the Missouri, but
whether going out or coming in it was impossible to tell in the dark. It was several days
old. This was discussed for some time. The

question was whether some had gone out in search of meat, or whether some additional men had come into camp.

"The Bunch of Stars was already a little west of the middle sky when we set out again. They agreed to take me a short distance beyond this creek and there leave me, as they were afraid to go any further. On the bank of the creek we took a farewell smoke. There was a faint glow in the east, showing that it was almost morning. The warriors sang a ' Strong Heart ' song for me in an undertone as I went on alone.

"I tried to make a wide circuit of the camp, but I passed their ponies grazing all over the side hills at a considerable distance, and I went as quietly as possible, so as not to frighten them. When I had fairly passed the camp I came down to the road again, and I let my horse fly!

"I had been cautioned at the post that the crossings of the creeks on either side of the camp were the most dangerous places, since they would be likely to watch for me there. I had left the second crossing far behind, and I felt quite safe; but I was tired and chilled by the long ride. My horse, too, began to show signs of fatigue. In a deep ravine where there was plenty of dry wood and shelter, I cleared the ground of snow and kindled a small fire. Then I gave the horse his last ration of oats, and I ate the last of the pemmican that the Ree scouts had given me.

"Suddenly he pricked up his ears in the direction of home. He ate a mouthful and listened again. I began to grow nervous, and I listened, too. Soon I heard the footsteps of horses in the snow at a considerable distance.

"Hastily I mounted and took flight along the ravine until I had to come out upon the open plain, in full view of a party of about thirty Sioux in war-paint, coming back from the direction of Fort Rice. They immediately gave chase, yelling and flourishing their guns and tomahawks over their heads. I urged my horse to his best speed, for I felt that if they should overtake me, nothing could save me! My friend, White Elk, here, was one of that war-party.

"I saw that I had a fair lead and the best

horse, and was gaining upon them, when about two miles out I met some more of the party who had lingered behind the rest. I was surrounded!

" I turned toward the north, to a deep gulch that I knew I should find there, and I led my horse along a narrow and slippery ridge to a deep hole. Here I took up my position. I guarded the pass with my bow and arrows, and they could not reach me unless they should follow the ridge in single file. I knew that they would not storm my position, for that is not the Indian way of fighting, but I supposed that they would try to tire me out. They yelled and hooted, and shot many bullets and arrows over my head to terrify me into surrender, but I remained motionless and silent.

" Night came, with a full round moon. All was light as day except the place where I stood, half frozen and not daring to move. The bottom of the gulch was as black as a well and almost as cold. The wolves howled all around me in the stillness.

" At last I heard the footsteps of horses retreating, and then no other sound. Still I dared not come out. I must have slept, for it was dawn when I seemed to hear faintly the yelling of warriors, and then I heard my own name.

" 'Zuyamani, tokiya nunka huwo?' (Where are you, Zuyamani?) they shouted. A party of my friends had come out to meet me and had followed our trail. I was scarcely able to walk when I came out, but they filled the pipe and held it up to me, as is done in recognition of distinguished service. They escorted me into the post, singing war songs and songs of brave deeds, and there I delivered up his letters to the Chief Soldier."

Again the drum was struck and the old men cheered Zuyamani, who added:

" I think that Poor Dog was right, for the Great Father never gave me any credit, nor did he ever reward me for what I had done. Yet I have not been without honor, for my own people have not forgotten me, even though I went upon the white man's errand."

VII

THE GRAVE OF THE DOG

THE full moon was just clear of the high mountain ranges. Surrounded by a ring of bluish haze, it looked almost as if it were frozen against the impalpable blue-black of the fleckless midwinter sky.

The game scout moved slowly homeward, well wrapped in his long buffalo robe, which was securely belted to his strong loins; his quiver tightly tied to his shoulders so as not to impede his progress. It was enough to carry upon his feet two strong snow-shoes; for the snow was deep and its crust too thin to bear his weight.

As he emerged from the lowlands into the upper regions, he loomed up a gigantic figure against the clear, moonlit horizon. His picturesque foxskin cap with all its trimmings was incrusted with frost from the breath of his nostrils, and his lagging footfall sounded crisply. The distance he had that day covered was enough for any human endurance; yet he was neither faint nor hungry; but his feet were frozen into the psay, the snow-shoes, so that he could not run faster than an easy slip and slide.

At last he reached the much-coveted point—the crown of the last ascent; and when he smelled fire and the savory odor of the jerked buffalo meat, it well-nigh caused him to waver! But he must not fail to follow the custom of untold ages, and give the game scout's wolf call before entering camp.

Accordingly he paused upon the highest point of the ridge and uttered a cry to which the hungry cry of a real wolf would have seemed but a coyote's yelp in comparison! Then it was that the rest of the buffalo hunters knew that their game scout was returning with welcome news; for the unsuccessful scout enters the camp silently.

A second time he gave the call to assure his hearers that their ears did not deceive them. The gray wolves received the news with perfect understanding. It meant food! " Woo-o-o-o! woo-o-o-o!" came from all directions, especially from the opposite ridge. Thus the ghostly, cold, weird night was enlivened with the music from many wild throats.

Down the gradual slope the scout hastened; his footfall was the only sound that broke the stillness after the answers to his call had ceased. As he crossed a little ridge an immense wolf suddenly confronted him, and instead of retreating, calmly sat up and gazed steadfastly into his face.

"Welcome, welcome, friend!" the hunter spoke as he passed.

In the meantime, the hunters at the temporary camp were aroused to a high pitch of excitement. Some turned their buffalo robes and put them on in such a way as to convert themselves into make-believe bison, and began to tread the snow, while others were singing the buffalo song, that their spirits might be charmed and allured within the circle of the camp-fires. The scout, too, was singing his buffalo bull song in a guttural, lowing chant as he neared the hunting camp. Within arrow-shot he paused again, while the usual ceremonies were enacted for his reception. This done, he was seated with the leaders in a chosen place.

"It was a long run," he said, "but there were no difficulties. I found the first herd directly north of here. The second herd, a great one, is northeast, near Shell Lake. The snow is deep. The buffalo can only follow their leader in their retreat."

"Hi, hi, hi!" the hunters exclaimed solemnly in token of gratitude, raising their hands heavenward and then pointing them toward the ground.

"Ho, kola! one more round of the buffalo-pipe, then we shall retire, to rise before daybreak for the hunt," advised one of the leaders. Silently they partook in turn of the long-stemmed pipe, and one by one, with a dignified "Ho!" departed to their teepees.

The scout betook himself to his little old buffalo teepee, which he used for winter hunting expeditions. His faithful Shunka, who had been all this time its only occupant, met him at the entrance as dogs alone know how to welcome a lifelong friend. As his master entered he stretched himself in his old-time way, from the tip of his tail to that of his tongue, and finished by curling both ends upward.

"Ho, mita shunka, eat this; for you must be hungry!" So saying, the scout laid before his canine friend the last piece of his dried buffalo meat. It was the sweetest meal ever eaten by a dog, judging by his long smacking of his lips after he had swallowed it!

The hunting party was soon lost in heavy slumber. Not a sound could be heard save the gnawing of the ponies upon the cottonwood bark, which was provided for them instead of hay in the winter time.

All about Shell Lake the bison were gathered in great herds. The unmistakable signs of the sky had warned them of approaching bad weather. The moon's robe was girdled with the rainbow wampum of heaven. The very music of the snow under their feet had given them warning. On the north side of Shell Lake there were several deep gulches, which were the homes of every wanderer of the plains at such a time at this. When there was a change toward severe weather, all the four-footed people headed for this lake. Here was a heavy growth of reeds, rushes, and coarse grass, making good shelters, and also springs, which afforded water after the lake was frozen solid. Hence great numbers of the bison had gathered here.

When Wapashaw, the game scout, had rolled himself in his warm buffalo robe and was sound asleep, his faithful companion hunter, the great Esquimaux wolf dog, silently rose and again stretched himself, then stood quiet for a moment as if meditating. It was clear that he knew well what he had planned to do, but was considering how he should do it without arousing any suspicion of his movements. This is a dog's art, and the night tricks and marauding must always be the joy and secret of his life!

Softly he emerged from the lodge and gave a sweeping glance around to assure him that there were none to spy upon him. Suspiciously he sniffed the air, as if to ascertain whether there could be any danger to his sleeping master while he should be away.

His purpose was still a secret. It may be that it was not entirely a selfish one, or merely the satisfying of his inherited traits. Having fully convinced himself of the safety of the unguarded camp, he went forth into the biting cold. The moon was now well up on the prairies of the sky. There were no cloud hills in the blue field above to conceal her from view. Her brilliant light set on fire every snow gem upon the plains and hillsides about the hunters' camp.

Up the long ascent he trotted in a northerly direction, yet not following his master's trail. He was large and formidable in strength, combining the features of his wild brothers of the plains with those of the dogs who keep company with the red men. His jet-black hair and sharp ears and nose appeared to immense advantage against the spotless and jeweled snow, until presently his own warm breath had coated him with heavy frost.

After a time Shunka struck into his master's trail and followed it all the way, only taking a short cut here and there when by dog instinct he knew that a man must go around such a point to get to his destination. He met many travelers during the night, but none had dared to approach him, though some few followed at a distance, as if to discover his purpose.

At last he reached Shell Lake, and there beheld a great gathering of the herds! They stood in groups, like enormous rocks, no longer black, but white with frost. Every one of them emitted a white steam, quickly frozen into a fine snow in the air.

Shunka sat upon his haunches and gazed. "Wough, this is it!" he said to himself. He had kept still when the game scout gave the wolf call, though the camp was in an uproar, and from the adjacent hills the wild hunters were equally joyous, because they understood the meaning of the unwonted noise. Yet his curiosity was not fully satisfied, and he had set out to discover the truth, and it may be to protect or serve his master in case of danger.

At daybreak the great dog meekly entered his master's rude teepee, and found him already preparing for the prospective hunt. He was filling his inside moccasins full of buffalo hair to serve as stockings, over which he put on his large buffalo moccasins with the hair inside, and adjusted his warm leggings. He then adjusted his snow-shoes and filled his quiver full of good arrows. The dog quietly lay down in a warm place, making himself as small as possible, as if to escape observation, and calmly watched his master.

"Ho, ho, ho, kola! Enákanee, enákanee!" shouted the game herald. "It is always best to get the game early; then their spirits can take flight with the coming of a new day!"

All had now donned their snow-shoes. There was no food left; therefore no delay to prepare breakfast.

"It is very propitious for our hunt," one exclaimed; "everything is in our favor. There is a good crust on the snow, and the promise of a good clear day!"

Soon all the hunters were running in single file upon the trail of the scout, each Indian closely followed by his trusty hunting dog. In less than two hours they stood just back of the low ridge which rounded the south side of Shell Lake. The narrow strip of land between its twin divisions was literally filled with the bison. In the gulches beyond, between the dark lines of timber, there were also scattered groups; but the hunters at once saw their advantage over the herd upon the peninsula.

"Hechetu, kola! This is well, friends!" exclaimed the first to speak. "These can be forced to cross the slippery ice and the mire around the springs. This will help us to get more meat. Our people are hungry, and we must kill many in order to feed them!"

"Ho, ho, ho!" agreed all the hunters.

"And it is here that we can use our companion hunters best, for the shunkas will intimidate and bewilder the buffalo women," said an old man.

"Ugh, he is always right! Our dogs must help us here. The meat will be theirs as well as ours," another added.

"Tosh, kola! The game scout's dog is the greatest shunka of them all! He has a mind near like that of a man. Let him lead the attack of his fellows, while we crawl up on the opposite side and surround the buffalo upon the slippery ice and in the deceitful mire," spoke up a third. So it was agreed that the game scout and his Shunka should lead the attack of the dogs.

THE GRAVE OF THE DOG

"Woo, woo, woo!" was the hoarse signal from the throat of the game scout; but his voice was drowned by the howling and barking of the savage dogs as they made their charge. In a moment all was confusion among the buffalo. Some started this way, others that, and the great mass swayed to and fro uncertainly. A few were ready to fight, but the snow was too deep for a countercharge upon the dogs, save on the ice just in front of them, where the wind had always full sweep. There all was slippery and shining! In their excitement and confusion the bison rushed upon this uncertain plain.

Their weight and the momentum of their rush carried them hopelessly far out, where they were again confused as to which way to go, and many were stuck in the mire which was concealed by the snow, except here and there an opening above a spring from which there issued a steaming vapor. The game scout and his valiant dog led on the force of canines with deafening war-cries, and one could see black heads here and there popping from behind the embankments. As the herd finally swept toward the opposite shore, many dead were left behind. Pierced by the arrows of the hunters, they lay like black mounds upon the glassy plain.

It was a great hunt! " Once more the camp will be fed," they thought, " and this good fortune will help us to reach the spring alive! "

A chant of rejoicing rang out from the opposite shore, while the game scout unsheathed his big knife and began the work which is ever the sequel of the hunt—to dress the game; although the survivors of the slaughter had scarcely disappeared behind the hills. The dogs had all run back to their respective masters, and this left the scout and his companion Shunka alone. Some were appointed to start a camp in a neighboring gulch among the trees, so that the hunters might bring their meat there and eat before setting out for the great camp on the Big River.

All were busily skinning and cutting up the meat into pieces convenient for carrying, when suddenly a hunter called the attention of those near him to an ominous change in the atmosphere.

THE GRAVE OF THE DOG

"There are signs of a blizzard! We must hurry into the near woods before it reaches us!" he shouted.

Some heard him; others did not. Those who saw or heard passed on the signal and hurried toward the wood, where others had already arranged rude shelters and gathered piles of dry wood for fuel.

Around the several camp-fires the hunters sat or stood, while slices of savory meat were broiled and eaten with a relish by the half-starved men.

"Ho, kola! Eat this, friend!" said they to one another as one finished broiling a steak of the bison and offered it to his neighbor.

But the storm had now fairly enveloped them in whirling whiteness. "Woo, woo!" they called to those who had not yet reached camp. One after another answered and emerged from the blinding pall of snow. At last none were missing save the game scout and his Shunka!

The hunters passed the time in eating and telling stories until a late hour, occasionally giving a united shout to guide the lost one should he chance to pass near their camp.

" Fear not for our scout, friends ! " finally exclaimed a leader among them. " He is a brave
and experienced man. He will find a safe rest-
ing-place, and join us when the wind ceases to
rage." So they all wrapped themselves in their
robes and lay down to sleep.

All that night and the following day it was
impossible to give succor, and the hunters felt
much concern for the absent. Late in the second
night the great storm subsided.

" Ho, ho ! Iyotanka ! Rise up ! " So the
first hunter to awaken aroused all the others.

As after every other storm, it was wonderfully
still; so still that one could hear distinctly the
pounding feet of the jack-rabbits coming down
over the slopes to the willows for food. All dry
vegetation was buried beneath the deep snow,
and everywhere they saw this white-robed creature of the prairie coming down to the woods.

Now the air was full of the wolf and coyote
game call, and they were seen in great numbers
upon the ice.

" See, see ! the hungry wolves are dragging
the carcasses away ! Harken to the war cries of

the scout's Shunka! Hurry, hurry!" they urged one another in chorus.

Away they ran and out upon the lake; now upon the wind-swept ice, now upon the crusted snow; running when they could, sliding when they must. There was certainly a great concourse of the wolves, whirling in frantic circles, but continually moving toward the farther end of the lake. They could hear distinctly the hoarse bark of the scout's Shunka, and occasionally the muffled war-whoop of a man, as if it came from under the ice!

As they approached nearer the scene they could hear more distinctly the voice of their friend, but still as it were from underground. When they reached the spot to which the wolves had dragged two of the carcasses of the buffalo, Shunka was seen to stand by one of them, but at that moment he staggered and fell. The hunters took out their knives and ripped up the frozen hide covering the abdominal cavity. It revealed a warm nest of hay and buffalo hair in which the scout lay, wrapped in his own robe!

He had placed his dog in one of the carcasses and himself in another for protection from the storm; but the dog was wiser than the man, for he kept his entrance open. The man lapped the hide over and it froze solidly, shutting him securely in. When the hungry wolves came Shunka promptly extricated himself and held them off as long as he could; meanwhile, sliding and pulling, the wolves continued to drag over the slippery ice the body of the buffalo in which his master had taken refuge. The poor, faithful dog, with no care for his own safety, stood by his imprisoned master until the hunters came up. But it was too late, for he had received more than one mortal wound.

As soon as the scout got out, with a face more anxious for another than for himself, he exclaimed:

" Where is Shunka, the bravest of his tribe? "

" Ho, kola, it is so, indeed; and here he lies," replied one sadly.

His master knelt by his side, gently stroking the face of the dog.

" Ah, my friend; you go where all spirits live!

The Great Mystery has a home for every living creature. May he permit our meeting there!"

At daybreak the scout carried him up to one of the pretty round hills overlooking the lake, and built up around him walls of loose stone. Red paints were scattered over the snow, in accordance with Indian custom, and the farewell song was sung.

Since that day the place has been known to the Sioux as Shunkahanakapi—the Grave of the Dog.

PART TWO

THE WOMAN

I

WINONA, THE WOMAN-CHILD

> Hush, hushaby, little woman!
> Be brave and weep not!
> The spirits sleep not;
> 'Tis they who ordain
> To woman, pain.
>
> Hush, hushaby, little woman!
> Now, all things bearing,
> A new gift sharing
> From those above—
> To woman, love.
>
> —*Sioux Lullaby.*

CHINTO, wéyanna! Yes, indeed; she is a real little woman," declares the old grandmother, as she receives and critically examines the tiny bit of humanity.

There is no remark as to the color of its hair or eyes, both so black as almost to be blue, but the old woman scans sharply the delicate profile of the baby face.

" Ah, she has the nose of her ancestors! Lips thin as a leaf, and eyes bright as stars in midwinter! " she exclaims, as she passes on the furry bundle to the other grandmother for her inspection.

" Tokee! she is pretty enough to win a twinkle from the evening star," remarks that smiling personage.

" And what shall her name be? "

" Winona, the First-born, of course. That is hers by right of birth."

" Still, it may not fit her. One must prove herself worthy in order to retain that honorable name."

" Ugh," retorts the first grandmother, " she can at least bear it on probation! "

" Tosh, tosh," the other assents.

Thus the unconscious little Winona has passed the first stage of the Indian's christening.

Presently she is folded into a soft white doeskin, well lined with the loose down of cattails, and snugly laced into an upright oaken cradle, the front of which is a richly embroidered buckskin bag, with porcupine quills and deers' hoofs suspended from its profuse fringes. This gay cradle is strapped upon the second grandmother's back, and that dignitary walks off with the newcomer.

"You must come with me," she says. "We shall go among the father and mother trees, and hear them speak with their thousand tongues, that you may know their language forever. I will hang the cradle of the woman-child upon Utuhu, the oak; and she shall hear the love-sighs of the pine maiden!"

In this fashion Winona is introduced to nature and becomes at once "nature-born," in accord with the beliefs and practices of the wild red man.

"Here she is! Take her," says the old woman on her return from the woods. She presents the child to its mother, who is sitting in the shade of an elm-tree as quietly as if she had not just passed through woman's severest ordeal in giving a daughter to the brave Chetonska!

"She has a winsome face, as meek and innocent as the face of an ermine," graciously adds the grandmother.

The mother does not speak. Silently and al-

most reverently she takes her new and first-born
daughter into her arms. She gazes into its velvety little face of a dusky red tint, and unconsciously presses the closely swaddled form to her
breast. She feels the mother-instinct seize upon
her strongly for the first time. Here is a new
life, a new hope, a possible link between herself
and a new race!

Ah, a smile plays upon her lips, as she realizes
that she has kissed her child! In its eyes and
mouth she discerns clearly the features she has
loved in the strong countenance of another,
though in the little woman's face they are softened and retouched by the hand of the " Great
Mystery."

The baby girl is called Winona for some
months, when the medicine-man is summoned
and requested to name publicly the first-born
daughter of Chetonska, the White Hawk; but
not until he has received a present of a good
pony with a finely painted buffalo-robe. It is
usual to confer another name besides that of
the " First-born," which may be resumed later
if the maiden proves worthy. The name Wi-

nona implies much of honor. It means charitable, kind, helpful; all that an eldest sister should be!

The herald goes around the ring of lodges announcing in singsong fashion the christening, and inviting everybody to a feast in honor of the event. A real American christening is always a gala occasion, when much savage wealth is distributed among the poor and old people. Winona has only just walked, and this fact is also announced with additional gifts. A wellborn child is ever before the tribal eye and in the tribal ear, as every little step in its progress toward manhood or womanhood—the first time of walking or swimming, first shot with bow and arrow (if a boy), first pair of moccasins made (if a girl)—is announced publicly with feasting and the giving of presents.

So Winona receives her individual name of Tatiyopa, or Her Door. It is symbolic, like most Indian names, and implies that the door of the bearer is hospitable and her home attractive.

The two grandmothers, who have carried the

little maiden upon their backs, now tell and sing to her by turns all the legends of their most noted female ancestors, from the twin sisters of the old story, the maidens who married among the star people of the sky, down to their own mothers. All her lullabies are feminine, and designed to impress upon her tender mind the life and duties of her sex.

As soon as she is old enough to play with dolls she plays mother in all seriousness and gravity. She is dressed like a miniature woman (and her dolls are clad likewise), in garments of doeskin to her ankles, adorned with long fringes, embroidered with porcupine quills, and dyed with root dyes in various colors. Her little blanket or robe, with which she shyly drapes or screens her head and shoulders, is the skin of a buffalo calf or a deer, soft, white, embroidered on the smooth side, and often with the head and hoofs left on.

"You must never forget, my little daughter, that you are a woman like myself. Do always those things that you see me do," her mother often admonishes her.

WINONA, THE WOMAN-CHILD

Even the language of the Sioux has its feminine dialect, and the tiny girl would be greatly abashed were it ever needful to correct her for using a masculine termination.

This mother makes for her little daughter a miniature copy of every rude tool that she uses in her taily tasks. There is a little scraper of elk-horn to scrape rawhides preparatory to tanning them, another scraper of a different shape for tanning, bone knives, and stone mallets for pounding choke-cherries and jerked meat.

While her mother is bending over a large buffalo-hide stretched and pinned upon the ground, standing upon it and scraping off the fleshy portion as nimbly as a carpenter shaves a board with his plane, Winona, at five years of age, stands upon a corner of the great hide and industriously scrapes away with her tiny instrument! When the mother stops to sharpen her tool, the little woman always sharpens hers also. Perhaps there is water to be fetched in bags made from the dried pericardium of an animal; the girl brings some in a smaller water-bag. When her mother goes for wood she carries one or two sticks on her back. She pitches her play teepee to form an exact copy of her mother's. Her little belongings are nearly all practical, and her very play is real!

Thus, before she is ten years old, Winona begins to see life honestly and in earnest; to consider herself a factor in the life of her people—a link in the genealogy of her race. Yet her effort is not forced, her work not done from necessity; it is normal and a development of the play-instinct of the young creature. This sort of training leads very early to a genuine desire to serve and to do for others. The little Winona loves to give and to please; to be generous and gracious. There is no thought of trafficking or economizing in labor and in love.

" Mother, I want to be like the beavers, the ants, and the spiders, because my grandmother says those are the people most worthy of imitation for their industry. She also tells me that I should watch the bee, the one that has so many daughters, and allows no young men to come around her daughters while they are at work making sweets," exclaims the little maiden.

"Truly their industry helps us much, for we often take from their hoard," remarks the mother.

"That is not right, is it mother, if they do not wish to share with us?" asks Winona. "But I think the bee is stingy if she has so much and will not share with any one else! When I grow up, I shall help the poor! I shall have a big teepee and invite old people often, for when people get old they seem to be always hungry, and I think we ought to feed them."

"My little daughter will please me and her father if she proves to be industrious and skillful with her needle and in all woman's work. Then she can have a fine teepee and make it all cheerful within. The indolent woman has a small teepee, and it is very smoky. All her children will have sore eyes, and her husband will soon become ill-tempered," declares the mother, in all seriousness.

"And, daughter, there is something more than this needed to make a cheerful home. You must have a good heart, be patient, and speak but little. Every creature that talks too much is sure to make trouble," she concludes, wisely.

One day this careful mother has completed a beautiful little teepee of the skin of a buffalo calf, worked with red porcupine quills in a row of rings just below the smoke-flaps and on each side of the front opening. In the center of each ring is a tassel of red and white horse-hair. The tip of each smoke-flap is decorated with the same material, and the doorflap also.

Within there are neatly arranged raw-hide boxes for housekeeping, and square bags of soft buckskin adorned with blue and white beads. On either side of the fireplace are spread the tanned skins of a buffalo calf and a deer; but there is no bear, wolf, or wildcat skin, for on these the foot of a woman must never tread! They are for men, and symbolical of manly virtues. There are dolls of all sizes, and a play travois leans against the white wall of the miniature lodge. Even the pet pup is called in to complete the fanciful home of the little woman.

" Now, my daughter," says the mother, " you must keep your lodge in order! "

Here the little woman is allowed to invite other little women, her playmates. This is where the grandmothers hold sway, chaperoning their young charges, who must never be long out of their sight. The little visitors bring their work-bags of various skins, artistically made and trimmed. These contain moccasins and other garments for their dolls, on which they love to occupy themselves.

The brightly-painted rawhide boxes are reserved for food, and in these the girls bring various prepared meats and other delicacies. This is perhaps the most agreeable part of the play to the chaperon, who is treated as an honored guest at the feast!

Winona seldom plays with boys, even her own brothers and cousins, and after she reaches twelve or fourteen years of age she scarcely speaks to them. Modesty is a virtue which is deeply impressed upon her from early childhood, and the bashfully drooping head, the averted look, the voice low and seldom heard, these are graces much esteemed in a maiden.

She is taught to pay great attention to the

care of her long, glossy locks, combing, plaiting, and perfuming them with sweet-scented leaves steeped in oil. Her personal appearance is well understood to be a matter of real moment, and rich dress and ornaments are highly prized. Fortunately they never go out of fashion, and once owned are permanent possessions, unless parted with as ceremonial gifts on some great occasion of mourning or festivity.

When she reaches a marriageable age her father allows her to give a feast to all the other girls of her immediate clan, and this " Feast of Virgins " may only be attended by those of spotless reputation. To have given or attended a number of them is regarded as a choice honor.

Tatiyopa, by the time she is fifteen, has already a name for skill in needlework, and generosity in distributing the articles of her own making. She is now generally called Winona— the charitable and kind! She believes that it is woman's work to make and keep a home that will be worthy of the bravest, and hospitable to all, and in this simple faith she enters upon the realities of her womanhood.

II

WINONA, THE CHILD-WOMAN

Braver than the bravest,
    You sought honors at death's door;
Could you not remember
    One who weeps at home—
Could you not remember me?

Braver than the bravest,
    You sought honors more than love;
Dear, I weep, yet I am not a coward;
    My heart weeps for thee—
My heart weeps when I remember thee!
                    —*Sioux Love Song.*

THE sky is blue overhead, peeping through window-like openings in a roof of green leaves. Right between a great pine and a birch tree their soft doeskin shawls are spread, and there sit two Sioux maidens amid their fineries—variously colored porcupine quills for embroidery laid upon sheets of thin birch-bark, and moccasin tops worked in colors like autumn leaves. It is Winona and her friend Miniyata.

They have arrived at the period during which the young girl is carefully secluded from her

brothers and cousins and future lovers, and re-
tires, as it were, into the nunnery of the woods,
behind a veil of thick foliage. Thus she is
expected to develop fully her womanly qualities.
In meditation and solitude, entirely alone or
with a chosen companion of her own sex and
age, she gains a secret strength, as she studies
the art of womanhood from nature herself.

Winona has the robust beauty of the wild
lily of the prairie, pure and strong in her deep
colors of yellow and scarlet against the savage
plain and horizon, basking in the open sun like
a child, yet soft and woman-like, with drooping head when observed. Both girls are beautifully robed in loose gowns of soft doeskin,
girded about the waist with the usual very wide
leather belt.

" Come, let us practice our sacred dance,"
says one to the other. Each crowns her glossy
head with a wreath of wild flowers, and they
dance with slow steps around the white birch,
singing meanwhile the sacred songs.

Now upon the lake that stretches blue to the
eastward there appears a distant canoe, a mere

speck, no bigger than a bird far off against the shining sky.

" See the lifting of the paddles! " exclaims Winona.

" Like the leaping of a trout upon the water! " suggests Miniyata.

" I hope they will not discover us, yet I would like to know who they are," remarks the other, innocently.

The birch canoe approaches swiftly, with two young men plying the light cedar paddles.

The girls now settle down to their needle-work, quite as if they had never laughed or danced or woven garlands, bending over their embroidery in perfect silence. Surely they would not wish to attract attention, for the two sturdy young warriors have already landed.

They pick up the canoe and lay it well up on the bank, out of sight. Then one procures a strong pole. They lift a buck deer from the canoe—not a mark upon it, save for the bullet wound; the deer looks as if it were sleeping! They tie the hind legs together and the fore legs also and carry it between them on the pole.

Quickly and cleverly they do all this; and now they start forward and come unexpectedly upon the maidens' retreat! They pause for an instant in mute apology, but the girls smile their forgiveness, and the youths hurry on toward the village.

Winona has now attended her first maidens' feast and is considered eligible to marriage. She may receive young men, but not in public or in a social way, for such was not the custom of the Sioux. When he speaks, she need not answer him unless she chooses.

The Indian woman in her quiet way preserves the dignity of the home. From our standpoint the white man is a law-breaker! The "Great Mystery," we say, does not adorn the woman above the man. His law is spreading horns, or flowing mane, or gorgeous plumage for the male; the female he made plain, but comely, modest and gentle. She is the foundation of man's dignity and honor. Upon her rests the life of the home and of the family. I have often thought that there is much in this philosophy of an untutored people. Had her husband

[184]

remained long enough in one place, the Indian woman, I believe, would have developed no mean civilization and culture of her own.

It was no disgrace to the chief's daughter in the old days to work with her hands. Indeed, their standard of worth was the willingness to work, but not for the sake of accumulation, only in order to give. Winona has learned to prepare skins, to remove the hair and tan the skin of a deer so that it may be made into moccasins within three days. She has a bone tool for each stage of the conversion of the stiff raw-hide into velvety leather. She has been taught the art of painting tents and raw-hide cases, and the manufacture of garments of all kinds.

Generosity is a trait that is highly developed in the Sioux woman. She makes many moccasins and other articles of clothing for her male relatives, or for any who are not well provided. She loves to see her brother the best dressed among the young men, and the moccasins especially of a young brave are the pride of his woman-kind.

Her own person is neatly attired, but ordinarily with great simplicity. Her doeskin gown has wide, flowing sleeves; the neck is low, but not so low as is the evening dress of society.

Her moccasins are plain; her leggins close-fitting and not as high as her brother's. She parts her smooth, jet-black hair in the middle and plaits it in two. In the old days she used to do it in one plait wound around with wampum. Her ornaments, sparingly worn, are beads, elks' teeth, and a touch of red paint. No feathers are worn by the woman, unless in a sacred dance.

She is supposed to be always occupied with some feminine pursuit or engaged in some social affair, which also is strictly feminine as a rule. Even her language is peculiar to her sex, some words being used by women only, while others have a feminine termination.

There is an etiquette of sitting and standing, which is strictly observed. The woman must never raise her knees or cross her feet when seated. She seats herself on the ground side-wise, with both feet under her.

Notwithstanding her modesty and undemonstrative ways, there is no lack of mirth and relaxation for Winona among her girl companions.

In summer, swimming and playing in the water is a favorite amusement. She even imitates with the soles of her feet the peculiar, resonant sound that the beaver makes with her large, flat tail upon the surface of the water. She is a graceful swimmer, keeping the feet together and waving them backward and forward like the tail of a fish.

Nearly all her games are different from those of the men. She has a sport of wand-throwing which develops fine muscles of the shoulder and back. The wands are about eight feet long, and taper gradually from an inch and a half to half an inch in diameter. Some of them are artistically made, with heads of bone and horn, so that it is remarkable to what a distance they may be made to slide over the ground. In the feminine game of ball, which is something like " shinny," the ball is driven with curved sticks between two goals. It is played with from two or three to a hundred on a side, and a game between two bands or villages is a picturesque event.

A common indoor diversion is the " deer's foot " game, played with six deer hoofs on a string, ending in a bone or steel awl. The object is to throw it in such a way as to catch one or more hoofs on the point of the awl, a feat which requires no little dexterity. Another is played with marked plum-stones in a bowl, which are thrown like dice and count according to the side that is turned uppermost.

Winona's wooing is a typical one. As with any other people, love-making is more or less in vogue at all times of the year, but more especially at midsummer, during the characteristic reunions and festivities of that season. The young men go about usually in pairs, and the maidens do likewise. They may meet by chance at any time of day, in the woods or at the spring, but oftenest seek to do so after dark, just outside the teepee. The girl has her companion, and he has his, for the sake of propriety or protection. The conversation is carried on in a whisper, so that even these chaperons do not hear.

At the sound of the drum on summer evenings, dances are begun within the circular rows of teepees, but without the circle the young men promenade in pairs. Each provides himself with the plaintive flute and plays the simple cadences of his people, while his person is completely covered with his fine robe, so that he cannot be recognized by the passer-by. At every pause in the melody he gives his yodel-like love-call, to which the girls respond with their musical, sing-song laughter.

Matosapa has loved Winona since the time he saw her at the lakeside in her parlor among the pines. But he has not had much opportunity to speak until on such a night, after the dances are over. There is no outside fire; but a dim light from within the skin teepees sheds a mellow glow over the camp, mingling with the light of a young moon. Thus these lovers go about like ghosts. Matosapa has already circled the teepees with his inseparable brother-friend, Brave Elk.

" Friend, do me an honor to-night! " he exclaims, at last. " Open this first door for me, since this will be the first time I shall speak to a woman! "

" Ah," suggests Brave Elk, " I hope you have selected a girl whose grandmother has no cross dogs! "

" The prize that is won at great risk is usually valued most," replies Matosapa.

" Ho, kola! I shall touch the door-flap as softly as the swallow alights upon her nest. But I warn you, do not let your heart beat too loudly, for the old woman's ears are still good! "

So, joking and laughing, they proceed toward a large buffalo tent with a horse's tail suspended from the highest pole to indicate the rank of the owner. They have ceased to blow the flute some paces back, and walk noiselessly as a panther in quest of a doe.

Brave Elk opens the door. Matosapa enters the tent. As was the wont of the Sioux, the well-born maid has a little teepee within a teepee—a private apartment of her own. He passes the sleeping family to this inner shrine.

There he gently wakens Winona with proper apologies. This is not unusual or strange to her innocence, for it was the custom of the people. He sits at the door, while his friend waits outside, and tells his love in a whisper. To this she does not reply at once; even if she loves him, it is proper that she should be silent. The lover does not know whether he is favorably received or not, upon this his first visit. He must now seek her outside upon every favorable occasion. No gifts are offered at this stage of the affair; the trafficking in ponies and " buying " a wife is entirely a modern custom.

Matosapa has improved every opportunity, until Winona has at last shyly admitted her willingness to listen. For a whole year he has been compelled at intervals to repeat the story of his love. Through the autumn hunting of the buffalo and the long, cold winter he often presents her kinsfolk with his game.

At the next midsummer the parents on both sides are made acquainted with the betrothal, and they at once begin preparations for the coming wedding. Provisions and delicacies of all

kinds are laid aside for a feast. Matosapa's
sisters and his girl cousins are told of the approaching event, and they too prepare for it,
since it is their duty to dress or adorn the bride
with garments made by their own hands.

With the Sioux of the old days, the great
natural crises of human life, marriage and birth,
were considered sacred and hedged about with
great privacy. Therefore the union is publicly
celebrated after and not before its consum-
mation. Suddenly the young couple disappear.
They go out into the wilderness together, and
spend some days or weeks away from the camp.
This is their honeymoon, away from all curious
or prying eyes. In due time they quietly return,
he to his home and she to hers, and now at last
the marriage is announced and invitations are
given to the feast.

The bride is ceremoniously delivered to her
husband's people, together with presents of rich
clothing collected from all her clan, which she
afterward distributes among her new relations.
Winona is carried in a travois handsomely decorated, and is received with equal ceremony.

WINONA, THE CHILD-WOMAN

For several days following she is dressed and painted by the female relatives of the groom, each in her turn, while in both clans the wedding feast is celebrated.

To illustrate womanly nobility of nature, let me tell the story of Dowanhotaninwin, Her-Singing-Heard. The maiden was deprived of both father and mother when scarcely ten years old, by an attack of the Sacs and Foxes while they were on a hunting expedition. Left alone with her grandmother, she was carefully reared and trained by this sage of the wild life.

Nature had given her more than her share of attractiveness, and she was womanly and winning as she was handsome. Yet she remained unmarried for nearly thirty years—a most unusual thing among us; and although she had worthy suitors in every branch of the Sioux nation, she quietly refused every offer.

Certain warriors who had distinguished themselves against the particular tribe who had made her an orphan, persistently sought her hand in marriage, but failed utterly.

One summer the Sioux and the Sacs and

Foxes were brought together under a flag of truce by the Commissioners of the Great White Father, for the purpose of making a treaty with them. During the short period of friendly intercourse and social dance and feast, a noble warrior of the enemy's tribe courted Dowan-hotaninwin.

Several of her old lovers were vying with one another to win her at the same time, that she might have inter-tribal celebration of her wedding.

Behold! the maiden accepted the foe of her childhood—one of those who had cruelly deprived her of her parents!

By night she fled to the Sac and Fox camp with her lover. It seemed at first an insult to the Sioux, and there was almost an outbreak among the young men of the tribe, who were barely restrained by their respect for the Commissioners of the Great Father.

But her aged grandfather explained the matter publicly in this fashion:

"Young men, hear ye! Your hearts are strong; let them not be troubled by the act of a young woman of your tribe! This has been her secret wish since she became a woman. She deprecates all tribal warfare. Her young heart never forgot its early sorrow; yet she has never blamed the Sacs and Foxes or held them responsible for the deed. She blames rather the customs of war among us. She believes in the formation of a blood brotherhood strong enough to prevent all this cruel and useless enmity. This was her high purpose, and to this end she reserved her hand. Forgive her, forgive her, I pray!"

In the morning there was a great commotion. The herald of the Sacs and Foxes entered the Sioux camp, attired in ceremonial garb and bearing in one hand an American flag and in the other a peace-pipe. He made the rounds singing a peace song, and delivering to all an invitation to attend the wedding feast of Dowanhotaninwin and their chief's son. Thus all was well. The simplicity, high purpose, and bravery of the girl won the hearts of the two tribes, and as long as she lived she was able to keep the peace between them.

III

SNANA'S FAWN

THE Little Missouri was in her spring fullness, and the hills among which she found her way to the Great Muddy were profusely adorned with colors, much like those worn by the wild red man upon a holiday! Looking toward the sunrise, one saw mysterious, deep shadows and bright prominences, while on the opposite side there was really an extravagant array of variegated hues. Between the gorgeous buttes and rainbow-tinted ridges there were narrow plains, broken here and there by dry creeks or gulches, and these again were clothed scantily with poplars and sad-colored bull-berry bushes, while the bare spots were purple with the wild Dakota crocuses.

Upon the lowest of a series of natural terraces there stood on this May morning a young Sioux girl, whose graceful movements were not unlike those of a doe which chanced to be lurking in a neighboring gulch. On the upper plains, not far away, were her young companions, all busily employed with the wewoptay, as it was called—the sharp-pointed stick with which the Sioux women dig wild turnips. They were gayly gossiping together, or each humming a love-song as she worked, only Snana stood somewhat apart from the rest; in fact, concealed by the crest of the ridge.

She had paused in her digging and stood facing the sun-kissed buttes. Above them in the clear blue sky the father sun was traveling upward as in haste, while to her receptive spirit there appealed an awful, unknown force, the silent speech of the Great Mystery, to which it seemed to her the whole world must be listening!

"O Great Mystery! the father of earthly things is coming to quicken us into life. Have pity on me, I pray thee! May I some day become the mother of a great and brave race of warriors!" So the maiden prayed silently.

It was now full-born day. The sun shone hot upon the bare ground, and the drops stood upon Snana's forehead as she plied her long pole. There was a cool spring in the dry creek bed near by, well hidden by a clump of choke-cherry bushes, and she turned thither to cool her thirsty throat. In the depths of the ravine her eye caught a familiar footprint—the track of a doe with the young fawn beside it. The hunting instinct arose within.

"It will be a great feat if I can find and take from her the babe. The little tawny skin shall be beautifully dressed by my mother. The legs and the nose shall be embossed with porcupine quills. It will be my work-bag," she said to herself.

As she stole forward on the fresh trail she scanned every nook, every clump of bushes. There was a sudden rustle from within a grove of wild plum trees, thickly festooned with grape and clematis, and the doe mother bounded away as carelessly as if she were never to return.

Ah, a mother's ruse! Snana entered the thorny enclosure, which was almost a rude tee-pee, and, tucked away in the furthermost corner, lay something with a trout-like, speckled, tawny coat. She bent over it. The fawn was apparently sleeping. Presently its eyes moved a bit, and a shiver passed through its subtle body.

"Thou shalt not die; thy skin shall not become my work-bag!" unconsciously the maiden spoke. The mother sympathy had taken hold on her mind. She picked the fawn up tenderly, bound its legs, and put it on her back to carry like an Indian babe in the folds of her robe.

"I cannot leave you alone, Tachinchala. Your mother is not here. Our hunters will soon return by this road, and your mother has left behind her two plain tracks leading to this thicket," she murmured.

The wild creature struggled vigorously for a minute, and then became quiet. Its graceful head protruded from the elkskin robe just over Snana's shoulder. She was slowly climbing the slope with her burden, when suddenly like an apparition the doe-mother stood before her. The fawn called loudly when it was first seized, and the mother was not too far away to hear. Now she called frantically for her child, at the same time stamping with her delicate fore-feet.

"Yes, sister, you are right; she is yours; but

[199]

you cannot save her to-day! The hunters will soon be here. Let me keep her for you; I will return her to you safely. And hear me, O sister of the woods, that some day I may become the mother of a noble race of warriors and of fine women, as handsome as you are!"

At this moment the quick eyes of the Indian girl detected something strange in the doe's actions. She glanced in every direction and behold! a grizzly bear was cautiously approaching the group from a considerable distance.

"Run, run, sister! I shall save your child if I can," she cried, and flew for the nearest scrub oak on the edge of the bank. Up the tree she scrambled, with the fawn still securely bound to her back. The grizzly came on with teeth exposed, and the doe-mother in her flight came between him and the tree, giving a series of indignant snorts as she ran, and so distracted Mato from his object of attack; but only for a few seconds—then on he came!

"Desist, O brave Mato! It does not become a great medicine-man to attack a helpless woman with a burden upon her back!"

Snana spoke as if the huge brute could understand her, and indeed the Indians hold that wild animals understand intuitively when appealed to by human beings in distress. Yet he replied only with a hoarse growl, as rising upon his hind legs he shook the little tree vigorously

" Ye, ye, heyupi ye! " Snana called loudl' to her companion turnip-diggers. Her cry soon brought all the women into sight upon a near-by ridge, and they immediately gave a general alarm. Mato saw them, but appeared not at all concerned and was still intent upon dislodging the girl, who clung frantically to her perch.

Presently there appeared upon the little knoll several warriors, mounted and uttering the usual war-whoop, as if they were about to swoop down upon a human enemy. This touched the dignity of Mato, and he immediately prepared to accept the challenge. Every Indian was alive to the possibilities of the occasion, for it is well known that Mato, or grizzly bear, alone among animals is given the rank of a warrior, so that whoever conquers him may wear an eagle feather.

"Woo! woo!" the warriors shouted, as they maneuvered to draw him into the open plain.

He answered with hoarse growls, threatening a rider who had ventured too near. But arrows were many and well-aimed, and in a few minutes the great and warlike Mato lay dead at the foot of the tree.

The men ran forward and counted their coups on him, just as when an enemy is fallen. Then they looked at one another and placed their hands over their mouths as the young girl descended the tree with a fawn bound upon her back.

"So that was the bait!" they cried. "And will you not make a feast with that fawn for us who came to your rescue?"

"The fawn is young and tender, and we have not eaten meat for two days. It will be a generous thing to do," added her father, who was among them.

"Ye-e-e!" she cried out in distress. "Do not ask it! I have seen this fawn's mother. I have promised to keep her child safe. See!

SNANA'S FAWN

I have saved its life, even when my own was in danger."

"Ho, ho, wakan ye lo! (Yes, yes, 'tis holy or mysterious)," they exclaimed approvingly.

It was no small trouble for Snana to keep her trust. As may well be supposed, all the dogs of the teepee village must be watched and kept at a distance. Neither was it easy to feed the little captive; but in gaining its confidence the girl was an adept. The fawn soon followed her everywhere, and called to her when hungry exactly as she had called to her own mother.

After several days, when her fright at the encounter with the bear had somewhat worn off, Snana took her pet into the woods and back to the very spot in which she had found it. In the furthest corner of the wild plum grove she laid it down, gently stroked its soft forehead, and smoothed the leaflike ears. The little thing closed its eyes. Once more the Sioux girl bent over and laid her cheek against the fawn's head; then reluctantly she moved away, hoping and yet dreading that the mother would return. She crouched under a clump of bushes near by, and gave the doe call. It was a reckless thing for her to do, for such a call might bring upon her a mountain lion or ever-watchful silver-tip; but Snana did not think of that.

In a few minutes she heard the light patter of hoofs, and caught a glimpse of a doe running straight toward the fawn's hiding-place. When she stole near enough to see, the doe and the fawn were examining one another carefully, as if fearing some treachery. At last both were apparently satisfied. The doe caressed her natural child, and the little one accepted the milk she offered.

In the Sioux maiden's mind there was turmoil. A close attachment to the little wild creature had already taken root there, contending with the sense of justice that was strong within her. Now womanly sympathy for the mother was in control, and now a desire to possess and protect her helpless pet.

"I can take care of her against all hunters, both animal and human. They are ever ready to seize the helpless fawn for food. Her life will be often exposed. You cannot save her from disaster. O, Takcha, my sister, let me still keep her for you!" she finally appealed to the poor doe, who was nervously watching the intruder, and apparently thinking how she might best escape with the fawn.

Just at this moment there came a low call from the wood. It was a doe call; but the wild mother and her new friend both knew that it was not the call of a real doe.

"It is a Sioux hunter!" whispered the girl. "You must go, my sister! Be off; I will take your child to safety!"

While she was yet speaking, the doe seemed to realize the danger. She stopped only an instant to lick fondly the tawny coat of the little one, who had just finished her dinner; then she bounded away.

As Snana emerged from the bushes with her charge, a young hunter met her face to face, and stared at her curiously. He was not of her father's camp, but a stranger.

"Ugh, you have my game."

"Tosh!" she replied coquettishly.

It was so often said among the Indians that

the doe was wont to put on human form to mis-
lead the hunter, that it looked strange to see
a woman with a fawn, and the young man could
not forbear to gaze upon Snana.

"You are not the real mother in maiden's
guise? Tell me truly if you are of human
blood," he demanded rudely.

"I am a Sioux maiden! Do you not know
my father?" she replied.

"Ah, but who is your father? What is his
name?" he insisted, nervously fingering his
arrows.

"Do not be a coward! Surely you should
know a maid of your own race," she replied re-
proachfully.

"Ah, you know the tricks of the doe! What
is thy name?"

"Hast thou forgotten the etiquette of thy
people, and wouldst compel me to pronounce
my own name? I refuse; thou art jesting!"
she retorted with a smile.

"Thou dost give the tricky answers of a doe.
I cannot wait; I must act before I lose my natural mind. But already I am yours. Whatever

purpose you may have in thus charming a poor hunter, be merciful," and, throwing aside his quiver, he sat down.

The maiden stole a glance at his face, and then another. He was handsome. Softly she reëntered the thicket and laid down the little fawn.

"Promise me never to hunt here again!" she said earnestly, as she came forth without her pretty burden, and he exacted another promise in return. Thus Snana lost her fawn, and found a lover.

IV

SHE-WHO-HAS-A-SOUL

I T was a long time ago, nearly two hundred years ago, that some of our people were living upon the shores of the Great Lake, Lake Superior. The chief of this band was called Tatankaota, Many Buffaloes.

One day the young son of Tatankaota led a war-party against the Ojibways, who occupied the country east of us, toward the rising sun.

When they had gone a day's journey in the direction of Sault Ste. Marie, in our language Skesketatanka, the warriors took up their position on the lake shore, at a point which the Ojibways were accustomed to pass in their canoes.

Long they gazed, and scanned the surface of the water, watching for the coming of the foe. The sun had risen above the dark pines, over the great ridge of woodland across the bay. It was the awakening of all living things. The birds were singing, and shining fishes leaped out of the water as if at play. At last, far off, there came the warning cry of the loon to stir their expectant ears.

"Warriors, look close to the horizon! This brother of ours does not lie. The enemy comes!" exclaimed their leader.

Presently upon the sparkling face of the water there appeared a moving canoe. There was but one, and it was coming directly toward them.

"Hahatonwan! Hahatonwan! (The Ojibways! the Ojibways!)" they exclaimed with one voice, and, grasping their weapons, they hastily concealed themselves in the bushes.

"Spare none—take no captives!" ordered the chief's son.

Nearer and nearer approached the strange canoe. The glistening blades of its paddles flashed as it were the signal of good news, or a welcome challenge. All impatiently waited until it should come within arrow-shot.

"Surely it is an Ojibway canoe," one murmured. "Yet look! the stroke is ungainly!"

Now, among all the tribes only the Ojibway's

art is perfect in paddling a birch canoe. This was a powerful stroke, but harsh and unsteady.

"See! there are no feathers on this man's head!" exclaimed the son of the chief. "Hold, warriors, he wears a woman's dress, and I see no weapon. No courage is needed to take his life, therefore let it be spared! I command that only coups (or blows) be counted on him, and he shall tell us whence he comes, and on what errand."

The signal was given; the warriors sprang to their feet, and like wolves they sped from the forest, out upon the white, sandy beach and straight into the sparkling waters of the lake, giving the shrill war-cry, the warning of death!

The solitary oarsman made no outcry—he offered no defense! Kneeling calmly in the prow of the little vessel, he merely ceased paddling and seemed to await with patience the deadly blow of the tomahawk.

The son of Tatankaota was foremost in the charge, but suddenly an impulse seized him to stop his warriors, lest one in the heat of excitement should do a mischief to the stranger. The canoe with its occupant was now very near, and it could be seen that the expression of his face was very gentle and even benignant. None could doubt his utter harmlessness; and the chief's son afterward declared that at this moment he felt a premonition of some event, but whether good or evil he could not tell.

No blows were struck—no coups counted. The young man bade his warriors take up the canoe and carry it to the shore; and although they murmured somewhat among themselves, they did as he commanded them. They seized the light bark and bore it dripping to a hill covered with tall pines, and overlooking the waters of the Great Lake.

Then the warriors lifted their war-clubs over their heads and sang, standing around the canoe in which the black-robed stranger was still kneeling. Looking at him closely, they perceived that he was of a peculiar complexion, pale and inclined to red. He wore a necklace of beads, from which hung a cross bearing the form of a man. His garments were strange, and most like the robes of woman. All of these things perplexed them greatly.

Presently the Black Robe told them by signs, in response to their inquiries, that he came from the rising sun, even beyond the Great Salt Water, and he seemed to say that he formerly came from the sky. Upon this the warriors believed that he must be a prophet or mysterious man.

Their leader directed them to take up again the canoe with the man in it, and appointed the warriors to carry it by turns until they should reach his father's village. This was done according to the ancient custom, as a mark of respect and honor. They took it up forthwith, and traveled with all convenient speed along the lake shore, through forests and across streams to a place called the Maiden's Retreat, a short distance from the village.

Thence the chief's son sent a messenger to announce to his father that he was bringing home a stranger, and to ask whether or not he should be allowed to enter the village. "His appearance," declared the scout, "is unlike that of any man we have ever seen, and his ways are mysterious!"

When the chief heard these words, he immediately called his council-men together to decide what was to be done, for he feared by admitting the mysterious stranger to bring some disaster upon his people. Finally he went out with his wisest men to meet his son's war-party. They looked with astonishment upon the Black Robe.

"Dispatch him! Dispatch him! Show him no mercy!" cried some of the council-men.

"Let him go on his way unharmed. Trouble him not," advised others.

"It is well known that the evil spirits sometimes take the form of a man or animal. From his strange appearance I judge this to be such a one. He should be put to death, lest some harm befall our people," an old man urged.

By this time several of the women of the village had reached the spot. Among them was She-who-has-a-Soul, the chief's youngest daughter, who tradition says was a maiden of much beauty, and of a generous heart. The stranger was evidently footsore from much travel and weakened by fasting. When she saw that the poor man clasped his hands and looked skyward as he uttered words in an unknown tongue, she pleaded with her father that a stranger who has entered their midst unchallenged may claim the hospitality of the people, according to the ancient custom.

"Father, he is weary and in want of food. Hold him no longer! Delay your council until he is refreshed!" These were the words of She-who-has-a-Soul, and her father could not refuse her prayer. The Black Robe was released, and the Sioux maiden led him to her father's teepee.

Now the warriors had been surprised and indeed displeased to find him dressed after the fashion of a woman, and they looked upon him with suspicion. But from the moment that she first beheld him, the heart of the maiden had turned toward this strange and seemingly unfortunate man. It appeared to her that great reverence and meekness were in his face, and with it all she was struck by his utter fearlessness, his apparent unconsciousness of danger.

The chief's daughter, having gained her father's permission, invited the Black Robe to his great buffalo-skin tent, and spreading a fine robe, she gently asked him to be seated. With the aid of her mother, she prepared wild rice sweetened with maple sugar and some broiled venison for his repast. The youthful warriors were astonished to observe these attentions, but the maiden heeded them not. She anointed the blistered feet of the holy man with perfumed otter oil, and put upon him a pair of moccasins beautifully worked by her own hands.

It was only an act of charity on her part, but the young men were displeased, and again urged that the stranger should at once be turned away. Some even suggested harsher measures; but they were overruled by the chief, softened by the persuasions of a well-beloved daughter.

During the few days that the Black Robe remained in the Sioux village he preached earnestly to the maiden, for she had been permitted to converse with him by signs, that she might try to ascertain what manner of man he was. He told her of the coming of a "Great

Prophet " from the sky, and of his words that he had left with the people. The cross with the figure of a man he explained as his totem which he had told them to carry. He also said that those who love him are commanded to go among strange peoples to tell the news, and that all who believe must be marked with holy water and accept the totem.

He asked by signs if She-who-has-a-Soul believed the story. To this she replied:

" It is a sweet story—a likely legend! I do believe ! "

Then the good father took out a small cross, and having pressed it to his heart and crossed his forehead and breast, he gave it to her. Finally he dipped his finger in water and touched the forehead of the maiden, repeating meanwhile some words in an unknown tongue.

The mother was troubled, for she feared that the stranger was trying to bewitch her daughter, but the chief decided thus:

" This is a praying-man, and he is not of our people; his customs are different, but they are not evil. Warriors, take him back to the spot where you saw him first! It is my desire, and the good custom of our tribe requires that you free him without injury!"

Accordingly they formed a large party, and carried the Black Robe in his canoe back to the shore of the Great Lake, to the place where they had met him, and he was allowed to depart thence whithersoever he would. He took his leave with signs of gratitude for their hospitality, and especially for the kindness of the beautiful Sioux maiden. She seemed to have understood his mission better than any one else, and as long as she lived she kept his queer trinket—as it seemed to the others—and performed the strange acts that he had taught her.

Furthermore, it was through the pleadings of She-who-has-a-Soul that the chief Tatankaota advised his people in after days to befriend the white strangers, and though many of the other chiefs opposed him in this, his counsels prevailed. Hence it was that both the French and English received much kindness from our people, mainly through the influence of this one woman!

[217]

OLD INDIAN DAYS

Such was the first coming of the white man
among us, as it is told in our traditions.   Other
praying-men came later, and many of the Sioux
allowed themselves to be baptized.   True, there
have been Indian wars, but not without reason;
and it is pleasant to remember that the Sioux
were hospitable to the first white "praying-
man," and that it was a tender-hearted maiden
of my people who first took in her hands the
cross of the new religion.

V

THE PEACE-MAKER

ONE of the most remarkable women of her day and nation was Eyatónkawee, She-whose-Voice-is-heard-afar. It is matter of history among the Wakpáykootay band of Sioux, the Dwellers among the Leaves, that when Eyatónkawee was a very young woman she was once victorious in a hand-to-hand combat with the enemy in the woods of Minnesota, where her people were hunting the deer. At such times they often met with stray parties of Sacs and Foxes from the prairies of Iowa and Illinois.

Now, the custom was among our people that the doer of a notable warlike deed was held in highest honor, and these deeds were kept constantly in memory by being recited in public, before many witnesses. The greatest exploit was that one involving most personal courage and physical address, and he whose record was adjudged best might claim certain privileges, not the least of which was the right to interfere in any quarrel and separate the combatants. The peace-maker might resort to force, if need be, and no one dared to utter a protest who could not say that he had himself achieved an equal fame.

There was a man called Tamáhay, known to Minnesota history as the " One-eyed Sioux," who was a notable character on the frontier in the early part of the nineteenth century. He was very reckless, and could boast of many a perilous adventure. He was the only Sioux who, in the War of 1812, fought for the Americans, while all the rest of his people sided with the British, mainly through the influence of the English traders among them at that time. This same " One-eyed Sioux " became a warm friend of Lieutenant Pike, who discovered the sources of the Mississippi, and for whom Pike's Peak is named. Some say that the Indian took his friend's name, for Tamáhay in English means Pike or Pickerel.

Unfortunately, in later life this brave man became a drunkard, and after the Americans took possession of his country almost any one of them would supply him with liquor in recognition of his notable services as a scout and soldier. Thus he was at times no less dangerous in camp than in battle.

Now, Eyatónkawee, being a young widow, had married the son of a lesser chief in Tamáhay's band, and was living among strangers. Moreover, she was yet young and modest.

One day this bashful matron heard loud warwhoops and the screams of women. Looking forth, she saw the people fleeing hither and thither, while Tamáhay, half intoxicated, rushed from his teepee painted for war, armed with tomahawk and scalping-knife, and approached another warrior as if to slay him. At this sight her heart became strong, and she quickly sprang between them with her woman's knife in her hand.

" It was a Sac warrior of like proportions and bravery with your own, who, having slain several of the Sioux, thus approached me with uplifted tomahawk ! " she exclaimed in a clear voice, and went on to recite her victory on that famous day so that the terrified people paused to hear.

Tamáhay was greatly astonished, but he was not too drunk to realize that he must give way at once, or be subject to the humiliation of a blow from the woman-warrior who challenged him thus. The whole camp was listening; and being unable, in spite of his giant frame and well-known record, to cite a greater deed than hers, he retreated with as good a grace as possible. Thus Eyatónkawee recounted her brave deed for the first time, in order to save a man's life. From that day her name was great as a peace-maker—greater even than when she had first defended so gallantly her babe and home!

Many years afterward, when she had attained middle age, this woman averted a serious danger from her people.

Chief Little Crow the elder was dead, and as he had two wives of two different bands, the succession was disputed among the half-brothers and their adherents. Finally the two sons of the wife belonging to the Wabashaw band plotted against the son of the woman of the

Kaposia band, His-Red-Nation by name, afterward called Little Crow—the man who led the Minnesota massacre.

They obtained a quantity of whisky and made a great feast to which many were invited, intending when all were more or less intoxicated to precipitate a fight in which he should be killed. It would be easy afterward to excuse themselves by saying that it was an accident.

Mendota, near what is now the thriving city of Saint Paul, then a queen of trading-posts in the Northwest, was the rendezvous of the Sioux. The event brought many together, for all warriors of note were bidden from far and near, and even the great traders of the day were present, for the succession to the chieftainship was one which vitally affected their interests. During the early part of the day all went well, with speeches and eulogies of the dead chief, flowing and eloquent, such as only a native orator can utter. Presently two goodly kegs of whisky were rolled into the council teepee.

Eyatónkawee was among the women, and

heard their expressions of anxiety as the voices
of the men rose louder and more threatening.
Some carried their children away into the woods
for safety, while others sought speech with their
husbands outside the council lodge and besought
them to come away in time. But more than
this was needed to cope with the emergency.
Suddenly a familiar form appeared in the door
of the council lodge.

" Is it becoming in a warrior to spill the blood
of his tribesmen? Are there no longer any
Ojibways? "

It was the voice of Eyatónkawee, that strong-
hearted woman! Advancing at the critical moment to the middle of the ring of warriors, she
once more recited her " brave deed " with all
the accompaniment of action and gesture, and
to such effect that the disorderly feast broke
up in confusion, and there was peace between
the rival bands of Sioux.

There was seldom a dangerous quarrel among
the Indians in those days that was not precipitated by the use of strong liquor, and this simple Indian woman, whose good judgment was

equal to her courage, fully recognized this fact. All her life, and especially after her favorite brother had been killed in a drunken brawl in the early days of the American Fur Company, she was a determined enemy to strong drink, and it is said did more to prevent its use among her immediate band than any other person. Being a woman, her sole means of recognition was the " brave deed " which she so wonderfully described and enacted before the people.

During the lifetime of She-whose-Voice-is-heard-afar—and she died only a few years ago —it behooved the Sioux men, if they drank at all, to drink secretly and in moderation. There are many who remember her brave entrance upon the scene of carousal, and her dramatic recital of the immortal deed of her youth.

" Hanta! hanta wo! (Out of the way!) " exclaim the dismayed warriors, scrambling in every direction to avoid the upraised arm of the terrible old woman, who bursts suddenly upon them with disheveled hair, her gown torn and streaked here and there with what looks like fresh blood, her leather leggins loose and

ungartered, as if newly come from the famous
struggle. One of the men has a keg of whisky
for which he has given a pony, and the others
have been invited in for a night of pleasure.
But scarcely has the first round been drunk to
the toast of " great deeds," when Eyatónkawee
is upon them, her great knife held high in her
wrinkled left hand, her tomahawk in the right.
Her black eyes gleam as she declaims in a voice
strong, unterrified:

"Look! look! brothers and husbands—the Sacs and Foxes
    are upon us!
  Behold, our braves are surprised—they are unprepared!
  Hear the mothers, the wives and the children screaming in
    affright!

"Your brave sister, Eyatónkawee, she, the newly made
    mother, is serving the smoking venison to her husband,
    just returned from the chase!
  Ah, he plunges into the thickest of the enemy!
  He falls, he falls, in full view of his young wife!

"She desperately presses her babe to her breast, while on they
    come yelling and triumphant!
  The foremost of them all enters her white buffalo-skin
    teepee:
  Tossing her babe at the warrior's feet, she stands before
    him, defiant;
  But he straightway levels his spear at her bosom.

THE PEACE-MAKER

Quickly she springs aside, and as quickly deals a deadly
    blow with her ax:
Falls at her feet the mighty warrior!

" Closely following on comes another, unknowing what fate
    has met his fellow!
He too enters her teepee, and upon his feather-decked head
    her ax falls—
Only his death-groan replies!

" Another of heroic size and great prowess, as witnessed by
    his war-bonnet of eagle-feathers,
Rushes on, yelling and whooping—for they believe that
    victory is with them!
The third great warrior who has dared to enter Eyatónka-
    wee's teepee uninvited, he has already dispatched her
    husband!
He it is whose terrible war-cry has scattered her sisters
    among the trees of the forest!

" On he comes with confidence and a brave heart, seeking
    one more bloody deed—
One more feather to win for his head!
Behold, he lifts above her woman's head his battle-ax!
No hope, no chance for her life! . . .
Ah! he strikes beyond her—only the handle of the ax falls
    heavily upon her tired shoulder!
Her ready knife finds his wicked heart,—
Down he falls at her feet!

" Now the din of war grows fainter and further.
The Sioux recover heart, and drive the enemy headlong
    from their lodges:
Your sister stands victorious over three!

[227]

"She takes her baby boy, and makes him count with his tiny
 hands the first 'coup' on each dead hero;
Hence he wears the 'first feathers' while yet in his oaken
 cradle.

"The bravest of the whole Sioux nation have given the war-
 whoop in your sister's honor, and have said:
'"Tis Eyatónkawee who is not satisfied with downing the
 mighty oaks with her ax—
She took the mighty Sacs and Foxes for trees, and she felled
 them with a will!'"

In such fashion the old woman was wont to
chant her story, and not a warrior there could
tell one to surpass it! The custom was strong,
and there was not one to prevent her when she
struck open with a single blow of her ax the keg
of whisky, and the precious liquor trickled upon
the ground.

"So trickles under the ax of Eyatónkawee the
blood of an enemy to the Sioux!"

VI

BLUE SKY

MANY years ago a large body of the Sioux were encamped at midsummer in the valley of the Cheyenne. It was customary at that period for the Indians to tie up their ponies over night within the circle of the teepees, whenever they were in disputed territory, for they considered it no wrong to steal the horses of the enemy. Hence this long procession of young men and maidens, returning at sunset to the camp with great bundles of green grass hanging gracefully from their saddles!

The " green grass parade " became a regular custom, and in fact a full-dress affair, since it was found to afford unusual opportunities for courtship.

Blue Sky, the pretty daughter of the Sioux chief, put on her best doeskin gown trimmed with elks' teeth, and investing her favorite spotted pony with his beaded saddle-blanket, she went forth in company with one of her maiden friends. Soon two young warriors overtook the pair; and as they approached they covered their heads with their robes, exposing only the upper part of the face disguised with paint and the single eagle feather standing upright. One carried a bow and quiver full of arrows; the other, a war-club suspended from his right arm.

"Ah, hay, hun, hay!" saluted one of them; but the modest maidens said never a word! It was not their way to speak; only the gay calico ponies pranced about and sportively threw back their ears to snap at the horses of the two young men.

"'Tis a brave welcome your horses are giving us!" he continued, while the two girls merely looked at one another with perfect understanding.

Presently Matoska urged his pony close to the Blue Sky's side.

"It may be that I am overbold," he murmured in her ear, "to repeat so soon my tale of love! I know well that I risk a reprimand, if not in words, then by a look or action!"

He paused to note the effect of his speech; but alas! it is the hard rule of savage courtship that the maiden may with propriety and dignity keep silence as long as she wishes, and it is often exasperatingly long.

"I have spoken to no maiden," he resumed, "because I wished to win the war-bonnet before doing so. But to you I was forced to yield!" Again he paused, as if fearing to appear unduly hasty; but deliberate as were speech and manner, his eyes betrayed him. They were full of intense eagerness mingled with anxiety.

"Sometimes I have imagined that I am in the world with you alone, traveling over the prairie of life, or sitting in our lonely white teepee, as the oriole sits with his mate before their swaying home. Yet I seemed to be never lonely, because you were there!" He finished his plea, and with outward calmness awaited her reply.

The maiden had not lost a word, but she was still thinking. She thought that a man is much like the wind of the north, only pleasant and comfortable in midsummer! She feared that she might some time have to furnish all the fuel for their love's fires; therefore she held her peace. Matoska waited for several minutes and them silently withdrew, bearing his disappointment with dignity.

Meanwhile the camp was astir with the returning youths and maidens, their horses' sides fringed with the long meadow grass, singing plaintive serenades around the circular rows of teepees before they broke up for the night.

It was a clear and quiet night; the evening fires were kindled and every teepee transformed into an immense Chinese lantern. There was a glowing ring two miles in circumference, with the wooded river bottom on one side and the vast prairie on the other. The Black Hills loomed up in the distance, and the rapids of the wild Cheyenne sent forth a varying peal of music on the wind. The people enjoyed their evening meal, and in the pauses of their talk and laughter the ponies could be heard munching at the bundles of green grass just outside the teepees.

Suddenly a chorus of yells broke cruelly the peace of the camp, followed by the dashing charge of the Crow Indian horsemen! It was met as bravely and quickly by the Sioux; and in the clear, pale moonlight the dusky warriors fought, with the occasional flash of a firearm, while silent weapons flew thick in the air like dragon-flies at sunset.

The brave mothers, wives, and sisters gave their shrill war-cry to inspire their men, and show the enemy that even the Sioux women cannot be daunted by such a fearful surprise!

When the morning sun sent its golden shafts among the teepees, they saw it through glistening tears—happy tears, they said, because the brave dead had met their end in gallant fight —the very end they craved! And among those who fell that night was Brave Hawk, the handsome brother of the Blue Sky.

In a few days the camp was moved to a point further up the Cheyenne and deeper into the bosom of the hills, leaving behind the decorated grave lodges belonging to the honored dead. A great council teepee was pitched, and here the people met to credit those who had earned them with the honors of the fight, that they might thereafter wear the eagle feathers which they had won.

"The first honor," declared the master of ceremonies, "belongs to Brave Hawk, who fell in the battle! He it was who compelled the Crows to retreat, when he bravely charged upon them and knocked from his horse the Crow chief, their war leader."

"Ho, it is true!" exclaimed the warriors in chorus.

"The second honor," he resumed, "belongs to Matoska, the White Bear!"

"Hun, hun, hay!" interposed another, "it is I, Red Owl, who touched the body of the Crow chief second to Brave Hawk!"

It was a definite challenge.

"The warriors who witnessed the act give the coup to Matoska, friend!" persisted the spokesman.

Red Owl was a brave youth and a close rival of Matoska, both for war honors and for the hand of the prettiest maiden in the tribe. He had hoped to be recognized as one who fought in defense of their homes by the side of Brave Hawk; that would please the Blue Sky, he thought; but the honor was conferred upon his rival!

There was a cloud of suppressed irritation on his dusky face as he sullenly departed to his own tent—an action which displeased the council-men. Matoska had not spoken, and this caused him to appear to the better advantage. The worst of it was that Blue Sky herself had entered the ring with the " orphan steed," as it was called—the war-horse of her dead brother, and had therefore seen and heard everything! Tanagila, or Hummingbird, the beautiful charger, decorated according to custom with the honors won by his master, was led away by the girl amidst resounding war-whoops.

Unable to remain quiet, Red Owl went out into the hills to fast and pray. It was sunset of the next day when he again approached the village, and behind a little ridge came suddenly upon Matoska and the girl standing together. It was the first time that they had met since the " green grass parade," and now only by accident, as the sister of Brave Hawk was in deep mourning. However, the lover had embraced his opportunity, and the maiden had said that she was willing to think of the matter. No more words were spoken.

That very night the council drum was struck three times, followed by the warriors' cheer. Everybody knew what that meant. It was an invitation to the young men to go upon the war-path against the Crows!

Blue Sky was unconsciously startled by this sudden announcement. For the first time in her life she felt a fear that she could not explain. The truth was that she loved, and was not yet fully aware of it. In spite of her fresh grief, she had been inexplicably happy since her last meeting with Matoska, for she had seen in him that which is so beautiful, so compelling in man to the eyes of the woman who loves. He, too, now cherished a real hope, and felt as if he could rush into the thickest of the battle to avenge the brother of his beloved!

In a few days the war-party had reached the

Big Horn and sent out advance scouts, who reported a large Crow encampment. Their hundreds of horses covered the flats like a great herd of buffalo, they said. It was immediately decided to attack at daybreak, and on a given signal they dashed impetuously upon the formidable camp. Some stampeded and drove off a number of horses, while the main body plunged into the midst of the Crows.

But the enemy were not easily surprised. They knew well the Sioux tactics, and there was a desperate struggle for supremacy. War-club was raised against war-club, and the death-song of the arrow filled the air! Presently the Sioux were forced to retreat, with the Crows in hot pursuit, like wolves after their prey.

Red Owl and Matoska had been among the foremost in the charge, and now they acted as a rear-guard, bravely defending the retreat of their little army, to the admiration of the enemy. At last a Crow raised his spear against Matoska, who in a flash dismounted him with a stroke of his oaken bow; but alas! the blow snapped the bow-string and left him defenseless. At the same instant his horse uttered a scream and fell, throwing its rider headlong!

There was no one near except Red Owl, who clapped his heels to his pony and joined in the retreat, leaving Matoska behind. He arose, threw down his quiver, and advanced alone to meet the oncoming rush of the Crows!

The Sioux had seen him fall. In a few moments he was surrounded by the enemy, and they saw him no more.

The pursuit was stopped, and they paused upon a hilltop to collect the remnant of their force. Red Owl was the last to come up, and it was observed that he did not look like himself.

" Tell us, what were Matoska's last words? " they asked him.

But he silently dismounted and sent an arrow through his faithful steed, to the astonishment of the warriors. Immediately afterward he took out his knife and stabbed himself to the heart.

" Ah! " they exclaimed, " he could not live to share our humiliation! "

The war-party returned defeated and cast

down by this unexpected ending to their adventure, having lost some of their bravest and best men. The camp was instantly thrown into mourning. Many were in heavy grief, but none was more deeply stricken than the maiden called the Blue Sky, the daughter of their chief.

She remained within her teepee and wept in secret, for none knew that she had the right to mourn. Yet she believed that her lover had met with misfortune, but not death. Although his name was announced among those warriors who fell in the field, her own heart assured her that it was not so. " I must go to him," she said to herself. " I must know certainly whether he is still among the living! "

The next evening, while the village was yet in the confusion of great trouble and sorrow, Blue Sky rode out upon her favorite pony as if to take him to water as usual, but none saw her return! She hastened to the spot where she had concealed two sacks of provisions and her extra moccasins and materials for sewing. She had no weapon, save her knife and a small hatchet. She knew the country between the

Black Hills and the Big Horn, and knew that it was full of perils for man and much more for woman. Yet by traveling only at night and concealing herself in the daytime she hoped to avoid these dangers, and she rode bravely forth on the trail of the returning warriors.

Her dog, Wapayna, had followed the maiden, and she was not sorry to have so faithful a companion. She cautioned him not to bark at or attack strange animals unless they attacked first, and he seemed to understand the propriety of remaining on guard whenever his mistress was asleep.

She reached the Powder River country in safety, and here she had more than once to pick her way among the buffaloes. These wily animals seemed to realize that she was only a woman and unarmed, so that they scarcely kept out of her path. She also crossed the trails of riders, some of them quite fresh, but was fortunate enough not to meet any of them.

At last the maiden attained the divide between the Tongue and the Big Horn rivers. Her heart beat fast, and the sudden sense of her strange mission almost overwhelmed her. She remembered the only time in her life that the Sioux were upon that river, and so had that bit of friendly welcome from the valley—a recollection of childhood!

It was near morning; the moon had set and for a short time darkness prevailed, but the girl's eyes had by this time become accustomed to the dark. She knew the day was at hand, and with its first beams she was safely tucked into one of those round turns left by the river long ago in changing its bed, now become a little grassy hollow sheltered by steep banks, and hidden by a fringe of trees. Here she picketed her pony, and took her own rest. Not until the afternoon shadows were long did she awake and go forth with determination to seek for the battlefield and for the Crow encampment.

It was not long before she came upon the bodies of fallen horses and men. There was Matoska's white charger, with a Sioux arrow in his side, and she divined the treachery of Red Owl! But he was dead, and his death had atoned for the crime. The body of her lover was nowhere to be found; yet how should they have taken the bravest of the Sioux a captive?

" If he had but one arrow left, he would stand and fight! If his bow-string were broken, he would still welcome death with a strong heart," she thought.

The evening was approaching and the Crow village in plain sight. Blue Sky arranged her hair and dress as well as she could like that of a Crow woman, and with an extra robe she made for herself a bundle that looked as if it held a baby in its many wrappings. The community was still celebrating its recent victory over the Sioux, and the camp was alive with songs and dances. In the darkness she approached unnoticed, and singing in an undertone a Crow lullaby, walked back and forth among the lodges, watching eagerly for any signs of him she sought.

At last she came near to the council lodge. There she beheld his face like an apparition through the dusk and the fire-light! He was sitting within, dressed in the gala costume of a Crow.

"O, he is living! he is living!" thought the brave maiden. "O, what shall I do?" Unconsciously she crept nearer and nearer, until the sharp eyes of an Indian detected the slight difference in her manner and dress, and he at once gave the alarm.

"Wah, wah! Epsaraka! Epsaraka! A Sioux! A Sioux!"

In an instant the whole camp had surrounded the girl, who stood in their midst a prisoner, yet undaunted, for she had seen her lover, and the spirit of her ancestors rose within her.

An interpreter was brought, a man who was half Crow and half Sioux.

"Young and pretty daughter of the Sioux!" exclaimed the chief, "tell us how you came here in our midst undetected, and why!"

"Because," replied the Blue Sky, "your brave warriors have slain my only brother, and captured my lover, whom you now hold a prisoner. It is for his sake that I have thus risked my life and honor!"

"Ho, ho! You are the bravest woman I have ever seen. Your lover was betrayed into our hands by the treachery of one of his own tribe, who shot his horse from behind. He faced us without fear, but it was not his courage that saved his life. He resembles my own son, who lately fell in battle, and according to the custom I have adopted him as my son!"

Thus the brave maiden captured the heart of the wily Crow, and was finally allowed to return home with her lover, bearing many and rich presents. Her name is remembered among the two tribes, for this act of hers resulted in a treaty of peace between them which was kept for a generation.

VII

THE FAITHFULNESS OF LONG EARS

AWAY beyond the Thin Hills, above the Big Lone Tree upon the Powder River, the Uncpapa Sioux had celebrated their Sun Dance, some forty years ago. It was midsummer and the red folk were happy. They lacked for nothing. The yellowish green flat on either side of the Powder was studded with wild flowers, and the cottonwood trees were in full leaf. One large circle of buffalo skin teepees formed the movable village. The Big Horn Mountains loomed up against the deep blue sky to the westward, and the Black Hills appeared in the far southeast.

The tribal rites had all been observed, and the usual summer festivities enjoyed to the full. The camp as it broke up divided itself in three parts, each of which had determined to seek a favorite hunting-ground.

One band journeyed west, toward the Tongue River. One followed a tributary of the Powder to the south. The third merely changed camp, on account of the grazing for ponies, and for four days remained near the old place.

The party that went west did not fail to realize the perilous nature of their wanderings, for they were trespassing upon the country of the warlike Crows.

On the third day at sunrise, the Sioux crier's voice resounded in the valley of the Powder, announcing that the lodges must be razed and the villagers must take up their march.

Breakfast of jerked buffalo meat had been served and the women were adjusting their packs, not without much chatter and apparent confusion. Weeko (Beautiful Woman), the young wife of the war-chief Shunkaska, who had made many presents at the dances in honor of her twin boys, now gave one of her remaining ponies to a poor old woman whose only beast of burden, a large dog, had died during the night.

This made it necessary to shift the packs of the others. Nakpa, or Long Ears, her kittenlike gray mule, which had heretofore been honored with the precious burden of the twin babies, was to be given a heavier and more cumbersome load. Weeko's two-year-old spotted pony was selected to carry the babies.

Accordingly, the two children, in their gorgeously beaded buckskin hoods, were suspended upon either side of the pony's saddle. As Weeko's first-born, they were beautifully dressed; even the saddle and bridle were daintily worked by her own hands.

The caravan was now in motion, and Weeko started all her ponies after the leader, while she adjusted the mule's clumsy burden of kettles and other household gear. In a moment:

"Go on, let us see how you move with your new load! Go on!" she exclaimed again, with a light blow of the horse-hair lariat, as the animal stood perfectly still.

Nakpa simply gave an angry side glance at her load and shifted her position once or twice. Then she threw herself headlong into the air and landed stiff-legged, uttering at the same time her unearthly protest. First she dove straight through the crowd, then proceeded in a circle, her heels describing wonderful curves and sweeps in the air. Her pack, too, began to come to pieces and to take forced flights from her undignified body and heels, in the midst of the screams of women and children, the barking of dogs, and the war-whoops of the amused young braves.

The cowskin tent became detached from her saddle, and a moment later Nakpa stood free. Her sides worked like a bellows as she stood there meekly indignant, apparently considering herself to be the victim of an uncalled-for mis-understanding.

" I should put an arrow through her at once, only she is not worth a good arrow," said Shunkaska, or White Dog, the husband of Weeko. At his wife's answer, he opened his eyes in surprised displeasure.

" No, she shall have her own pack again. She wants her twins. I ought never to have taken them from her ! "

Weeko approached Nakpa as she stood alone

and unfriended in the face of her little world, all of whom considered that she had committed the unpardonable sin. As for her, she evidently felt that her misfortunes had not been of her own making. She gave a hesitating, sidelong look at her mistress.

"Nakpa, you should not have acted so. I knew you were stronger than the others, therefore I gave you that load," said Weeko in a conciliatory tone, and patted her on the nose. "Come, now, you shall have your own pet pack," and she led her back to where the young pony stood silently with the babies.

Nakpa threw back her ears and cast savage looks at him, while Shunkaska, with no small annoyance, gathered together as much as he could of their scattered household effects. The sleeping brown-skinned babies in their chrysalis-like hoods were gently lowered from the pony's back and attached securely to Nakpa's padded wooden saddle. The family pots and kettles were divided among the pack ponies. Order was restored and the village once more in motion.

" Come now, Nakpa; you have your wish. You must take good care of my babies. Be good, because I have trusted you," murmured the young mother in her softest tones.

" Really, Weeko, you have some common ground with Nakpa, for you both always want to have your own way, and stick to it, too! I tell you, I fear this Long Ears. She is not to be trusted with babies," remarked Shunkaska, with a good deal of severity.

But his wife made no reply, for she well knew that though he might criticise, he would not actually interfere with her domestic arrangements.

He now started ahead to join the men in advance of the slow-moving procession, thus leaving her in undivided charge of her household. One or two of the pack ponies were not well-trained and required all her attention. Nakpa had been a faithful servant until her escapade of the morning, and she was now obviously satisfied with her mistress' arrangements. She walked alongside with her lariat dragging, and perfectly free to do as she pleased.

Some hours later, the party ascended a slope from the river bottom to cross over the divide which lay between the Powder River and a tributary stream. They had hitherto followed that river in a westerly direction, but here it took its course southward, winding in a blue streak until lost to view among the foot-hills of the Big Horn Mountains. The ford was deep, with a swift current. Here and there a bald butte stood out in full relief against the brilliant blue sky. The Sioux followed a deep ravine until they came almost up to the second row of terraces.

"Whoo! whoo!" came the blood-curdling signal of danger from the front. It was no unfamiliar sound—the rovers knew it only too well. It meant sudden death—or at best a cruel struggle and frantic flight.

Terrified, yet self-possessed, the women turned to fly while yet there was time. Instantly the mother looked to Nakpa, who carried on either side of the saddle her precious boys. She hurriedly examined the fastenings to see that all was secure, and then caught her swiftest

[251]

pony, for, like all Indian women, she knew just what was happening, and that while her husband was engaged in front with the enemy, she must seek safety with her babies.

Hardly was she in the saddle when a heart-rending war-whoop sounded on their flank, and she knew that they were surrounded! Instinctively she reached for her husband's second quiver of arrows, which was carried by one of the pack ponies. Alas! the Crow warriors were already upon them! The ponies became unmanageable, and the wild screams of women and children pierced the awful confusion.

Quick as a flash, Weeko turned again to her babies, but Nakpa had already disappeared!

Then, maddened by fright and the loss of her children, Weeko became forgetful of her sex and tenderness, for she sternly grasped her husband's bow in her left hand to do battle.

That charge of the Crows was a disastrous one, but the Sioux were equally brave and desperate. Charges and counter-charges were made, and the slain were many on both sides. The fight lasted until darkness came. Then the Crows departed and the Sioux buried their dead.

When the Crows made their flank charge, Nakpa apparently appreciated the situation. To save herself and the babies, she took a desperate chance. She fled straight through the attacking force.

When the warriors came howling upon her in great numbers, she at once started back the way she had come, to the camp left behind. They had traveled nearly three days. To be sure, they did not travel more than fifteen miles a day, but it was full forty miles to cover before dark.

"Look! look!" exclaimed a warrior, "two babies hung from the saddle of a mule!"

No one heeded this man's call, and his arrow did not touch Nakpa or either of the boys, but it struck the thick part of the saddle over the mule's back.

"Lasso her! lasso her!" he yelled once more; but Nakpa was too cunning for them. She dodged in and out with active heels, and they could not afford to waste many arrows on a mule at that stage of the fight. Down the ravine, then over the expanse of prairie dotted with gray-green sage-brush, she sped with her unconscious burden.

"Whoo! whoo!" yelled another Crow to his comrades, "the Sioux have dispatched a runner to get reinforcements! There he goes, down on the flat! Now he has almost reached the river bottom!"

It was only Nakpa. She laid back her ears and stretched out more and more to gain the river, for she realized that when she had crossed the ford the Crows would not pursue her farther.

Now she had reached the bank. With the intense heat from her exertions, she was extremely nervous, and she imagined a warrior beind every bush. Yet she had enough sense left to realize that she must not satisfy her thirst. She tried the bottom with her fore-foot, then waded carefully into the deep stream.

She kept her big ears well to the front as she swam to catch the slightest sound. As she stepped on the opposite shore, she shook herself and the boys vigorously, then pulled a few mouthfuls of grass and started on.

Soon one of the babies began to cry, and the other was not long in joining him. Nakpa did not know what to do. She gave a gentle whinny and both babies apparently stopped to listen; then she took up an easy gait as if to put them to sleep.

These tactics answered only for a time. As she fairly flew over the lowlands, the babies' hunger increased and they screamed so loud that a passing coyote had to sit upon his haunches and wonder what in the world the fleeing long-eared horse was carrying on his saddle. Even magpies and crows flew near as if to ascertain the meaning of this curious sound.

Nakpa now came to the Little Trail Creek, a tributary of the Powder, not far from the old camp. No need of wasting any time here, she thought. Then she swerved aside so suddenly as almost to jerk her babies out of their cradles. Two gray wolves, one on each side, approached her, growling low—their white teeth show-ing.

Never in her humble life had Nakpa been
in more desperate straits. The larger of the
wolves came fiercely forward to engage her
attention, while his mate was to attack her behind and cut her hamstrings. But for once the
pair had made a miscalculation. The mule used
her front hoofs vigorously on the foremost wolf,
while her hind ones were doing even more
effective work. The larger wolf soon went
limping away with a broken hip, and the one
in the rear received a deep cut on the jaw which
proved an effectual discouragement.

A little further on, an Indian hunter drew
near on horseback, but Nakpa did not pause or
slacken her pace. On she fled through the long
dry grass of the river bottoms, while her babies
slept again from sheer exhaustion. Toward
sunset, she entered the Sioux camp amid great
excitement, for some one had spied her afar
off, and the boys and the dogs announced her
coming.

"Whoo, whoo! Weeko's Nakpa has come
back with the twins! Whoo, whoo!" exclaimed
the men. "Tokee! tokee!" cried the women.

A sister to Weeko who was in the village came forward and released the children, as Nakpa gave a low whinny and stopped. Tenderly Zeezeewin nursed them at her own motherly bosom, assisted by another young mother of the band.

"Ugh, there is a Crow arrow sticking in the saddle! A fight! a fight!" exclaimed the warriors.

"Sing a Brave-Heart song for the Long-Eared one! She has escaped alone with her charge. She is entitled to wear an eagle's feather! Look at the arrow in her saddle! and more, she has a knife wound in her jaw and an arrow cut on her hind leg.—No, those are the marks of a wolf's teeth! She has passed through many dangers and saved two chief's sons, who will some day make the Crows sorry for this day's work!"

The speaker was an old man who thus addressed the fast gathering throng.

Zeezeewin now came forward again with an eagle feather and some white paint in her hands. The young men rubbed Nakpa down, and the feather, marked with red to indicate her wounds, was fastened to her mane. Shoulders and hips were touched with red paint to show her endurance in running. Then the crier, praising her brave deed in heroic verse, led her around the camp, inside of the circle of teepees. All the people stood outside their lodges and listened respectfully, for the Dakota loves well to honor the faithful and the brave.

During the next day, riders came in from the ill-fated party, bringing the sad news of the fight and heavy loss. Late in the afternoon came Weeko, her face swollen with crying, her beautiful hair cut short in mourning, her garments torn and covered with dust and blood. Her husband had fallen in the fight, and her twin boys she supposed to have been taken captive by the Crows. Singing in a hoarse voice the praises of her departed warrior, she entered the camp. As she approached her sister's teepee, there stood Nakpa, still wearing her honorable decorations. At the same moment, Zeezeewin came out to meet her with both babies in her arms.

[258]

THE FAITHFULNESS OF LONG EARS

"Mechinkshee! meechinkshee! (my sons, my sons!)" was all that the poor mother could say, as she all but fell from her saddle to the ground. The despised Long Ears had not betrayed her trust.

VIII

THE WAR MAIDEN

THE old man, Smoky Day, was for many years the best-known story-teller and historian of his tribe. He it was who told me the story of the War Maiden. In the old days it was unusual but not unheard of for a woman to go upon the war-path—perhaps a young girl, the last of her line, or a widow whose well-loved husband had fallen on the field—and there could be no greater incentive to feats of desperate daring on the part of the warriors.

"A long time ago," said old Smoky Day, "the Unkpapa and the Cut-Head bands of Sioux united their camps upon a vast prairie east of the Minne Wakan (now called Devil's Lake). It was midsummer, and the people shared in the happiness of every living thing. We had food in abundance, for bison in countless numbers overspread the plain.

"The teepee village was laid out in two great

rings, and all was in readiness for the midsummer entertainments. There were ball games, feasts and dances every day, and late into the night. You have heard of the festivities of those days; there are none like them now," said the old man, and he sighed heavily as he laid down the red pipe which was to be passed from hand to hand during the recital.

"The head chief of the Unkpapas then was Tamákoche (His Country). He was in his time a notable warrior, a hunter and a feast-maker, much beloved by his people. He was the father of three sons, but he was so anxious to make them warriors of great reputation that they had all, despising danger, been killed in battle.

"The chief had also a very pretty daughter, whose name was Makátah. Since all his sons were slain he had placed his affections solely upon the girl, and she grew up listening to the praises of the brave deeds of her brothers, which her father never tired of chanting when they were together in the lodge. At times Makátah was called upon to dance to the 'Strong-Heart' songs. Thus even as a child she loved the thought of war, although she was the prettiest and most modest maiden in the two tribes. As she grew into womanhood she became the belle of her father's village, and her beauty and spirit were talked of even among the neighboring bands of Sioux. But it appeared that Makátah did not care to marry. She had only two ambitions. One was to prove to her father that, though only a maid, she had the heart of a warrior. The other was to visit the graves of her brothers—that is, the country of the enemy.

" At this pleasant reunion of two kindred peoples one of the principal events was the Feast of Virgins, given by Makátah. All young maidens of virtue and good repute were invited to be present; but woe to her who should dare to pollute the sacred feast! If her right to be there were challenged by any it meant a public disgrace. The two arrows and the red stone upon which the virgins took their oath of chastity were especially prepared for the occasion. Every girl was beautifully dressed, for at that time the white doeskin gowns, with a profusion

of fringes and colored embroidery, were the
gala attire of the Sioux maidens. Red paint was
added, and ornaments of furs and wampum.
Many youths eagerly surveyed the maiden gathering, at which the daughter of Tamákoche out-
shone all the rest.

" Several eligible warriors now pressed their
suits at the chieftain's lodge, and among them
were one or two whom he would have gladly
called son-in-law; but no! Makátah would not
listen to words of courtship. She had vowed,
she said, to the spirits of her three brothers—
each of whom fell in the country of the Crows
—that she would see that country before she
became a wife.

" Red Horn, who was something of a leader
among the young men, was a persistent and determined suitor. He had urged every influential
friend of his and hers to persuade her to listen
to him. His presents were more valuable than
those of any one else. He even made use of
his father's position as a leading chief of the
Cut-Head band to force a decision in his favor;
and while the maiden remained indifferent her

father seemed inclined to countenance this young man's pretensions.

" She had many other lovers, as I have said," the old man added, " and among them was one Little Eagle, an orphan and a poor young man, unknown and unproved as a warrior. He was so insignificant that nobody thought much about him, and if Makátah regarded him with any favor the matter was her secret, for it is certain that she did not openly encourage him.

" One day it was reported in the village that their neighbors, the Cut-Head Sioux, would organize a great attack upon the Crows at the mouth of the Redwater, a tributary of the Missouri. Makátah immediately inquired of her male cousins whether any of them expected to join the war-party.

" ' Three of us will go,' they replied.

" ' Then,' said the girl, ' I beg that you will allow me to go with you! I have a good horse, and I shall not handicap you in battle. I only ask your protection in camp as your kinswoman and a maid of the war-party.'

" ' If our uncle Tamákoche sanctions your

going,' they replied, ' we shall be proud to have
our cousin with us, to inspire us to brave
deeds!'

" The maiden now sought her father and
asked his permission to accompany the war-
party.

" ' I wish,' said she, ' to visit the graves of my
brothers! I shall carry with me their war-bon-
nets and their weapons, to give to certain young
men on the eve of battle, according to the ancient custom. Long ago I resolved to do this,
and the time is now come.'

" The chief was at this time well advanced
in years, and had been sitting quite alone in his
lodge, thinking upon the days of his youth, when
he was noted for daring and success in battle.
In silence he listened as he filled his pipe, and
seemed to meditate while he smoked the fra-
grant tobacco. At last he spoke with tears in
his eyes.

" ' Daughter, I am an old man! My heart
beats in my throat, and my old eyes cannot keep
back the tears. My three sons, on whom I had
placed all my hopes, are gone to a far country!

You are the only child left to my old age, and you, too, are brave—as brave as any of your brothers. If you go I fear that you may not return to me; yet I cannot refuse you my permission!"

"The old man began to chant a war-song, and some of his people, hearing him, came in to learn what was in his mind. He told them all, and immediately many young men volunteered for the war-party, in order to have the honor of going with the daughter of their chief.

"Several of Makátah's suitors were among them, and each watched eagerly for an opportunity to ride at her side. At night she pitched her little teepee within the circle of her cousins' campfires, and there she slept without fear. Courteous youths brought to her every morning and evening fresh venison for her repast. Yet there was no courting, for all attentions paid to a maiden when on the war-path must be those of a brother to a sister, and all must be equally received by her.

"Two days later, when the two parties of Sioux met on the plains, the maiden's presence

was heralded throughout the camp, as an in-
spiration to the young and untried warriors of
both bands to distinguish themselves in the field.
It is true that some of the older men considered
it unwise to allow Makátah to accompany the
war-party.

" ' The girl,' said they to one another, ' is
very ambitious as well as brave. She will surely
risk her own life in battle, which will make the
young men desperate, and we shall lose many
of them ! '

" Nevertheless they loved her and her father;
therefore they did not protest openly.

" On the third day the Sioux scouts returned
with the word that the Crows were camping,
as had been supposed, at the confluence of the
Redwater and the Missouri Rivers. It was a
great camp. All the Crow tribe were there,
they said, with their thousands of fine horses.

" There was excitement in the Sioux camp,
and all of the head men immediately met in
council. It was determined to make the attack
early on the following morning, just as the sun
came over the hills. The councilors agreed that

in honor of the great chief, her father, as well as in recognition of her own courage, Makátah should be permitted to lead the charge at the outset, but that she must drop behind as they neared the enemy. The maiden, who had one of the fleetest ponies in that part of the country, had no intention of falling back, but she did not tell any one what was in her mind.

"That evening every warrior sang his war-song, and announced the particular war-charm or ' medicine ' of his clan, according to the custom. The youths were vying with one another in brave tales of what they would do on the morrow. The voice of Red Horn was loud among the boasters, for he was known to be a vain youth, although truly not without reputation. Little Eagle, who was also of the company, remained modestly silent, as indeed became one without experience in the field. In the midst of the clamor there fell a silence.

"'Hush! hush!' they whispered. 'Look, look! The War Maiden comes!'

"All eyes were turned upon Makátah, who rode her fine buckskin steed with a single lariat.

[268]

He held his head proudly, and his saddle was heavy with fringes and gay with colored embroidery. The maiden was attired in her best and wore her own father's war-bonnet, while she carried in her hands two which had belonged to two of her dead brothers. Singing in a clear voice the songs of her clan, she completed the circle, according to custom, before she singled out one of the young braves for special honor by giving him the bonnet which she held in her right hand. She then crossed over to the Cut-Heads, and presented the other bonnet to one of their young men. She was very handsome; even the old men's blood was stirred by her brave appearance!

" At daybreak the two war-parties of the Sioux, mounted on their best horses, stood side by side, ready for the word to charge. All of the warriors were painted for the battle—prepared for death—their nearly nude bodies decorated with their individual war-totems. Their well-filled quivers were fastened to their sides, and each tightly grasped his oaken bow.

" The young man with the finest voice had

been chosen to give the signal—a single high-pitched yell. This was an imitation of the one long howl of the gray wolf before he makes the attack. It was an ancient custom of our people.

" ' Woo-o-o-o! '—at last it came! As the sound ceased a shrill war-whoop from five hundred throats burst forth in chorus, and at the same instant Makátah, upon her splendid buckskin pony, shot far out upon the plain, like an arrow as it leaves the bow. It was a glorious sight! No man has ever looked upon the like again! "

The eyes of the old man sparkled as he spoke, and his bent shoulders straightened.

" The white doeskin gown of the War Maiden," he continued, " was trimmed with elk's teeth and tails of ermine. Her long black hair hung loose, bound only with a strip of otter-skin, and with her eagle-feather war-bonnet floated far behind. In her hand she held a long coup-staff decorated with eagle-feathers. Thus she went forth in advance of them all!

" War cries of men and screams of terrified

women and children were borne upon the clear morning air as our warriors neared the Crow camp. The charge was made over a wide plain, and the Crows came yelling from their lodges, fully armed, to meet the attacking party. In spite of the surprise they easily held their own, and even began to press us hard, as their number was much greater than that of the Sioux.

"The fight was a long and hard one. Toward the end of the day the enemy made a counter-charge. By that time many of our ponies had fallen or were exhausted. The Sioux retreated, and the slaughter was great. The Cut-Heads fled womanlike; but the people of Tamákoche fought gallantly to the very last.

"Makátah remained with her father's people. Many cried out to her, 'Go back! Go back!' but she paid no attention. She carried no weapon throughout the day—nothing but her coup-staff—but by her presence and her cries of encouragement or praise she urged on the men to deeds of desperate valor.

"Finally, however, the Sioux braves were

hotly pursued and the retreat became general. Now at last Makátah tried to follow; but her pony was tired, and the maiden fell farther and farther behind. Many of her lovers passed her silently, intent upon saving their own lives. Only a few still remained behind, fighting desperately to cover the retreat, when Red Horn came up with the girl. His pony was still fresh. He might have put her up behind him and carried her to safety, but he did not even look at her as he galloped by.

" Makátah did not call out, but she could not help looking after him. He had declared his love for her more loudly than any of the others, and she now gave herself up to die.

" Presently another overtook the maiden. It was Little Eagle, unhurt and smiling.

" ' Take my horse! ' he said to her. ' I shall remain here and fight! '

" The maiden looked at him and shook her head, but he sprang off and lifted her upon his horse. He struck him a smart blow upon the flank that sent him at full speed in the direction of the Sioux encampment. Then he seized the exhausted buckskin by the lariat, and turned back to join the rear-guard.

"That little group still withstood in some fashion the all but irresistible onset of the Crows. When their comrade came back to them, leading the War Maiden's pony, they were inspired to fresh endeavor, and though few in number they made a counter-charge with such fury that the Crows in their turn were forced to retreat!

"The Sioux got fresh mounts and returned to the field, and by sunset the day was won! Little Eagle was among the first who rode straight through the Crow camp, causing terror and consternation. It was afterward remembered that he looked unlike his former self and was scarcely recognized by the warriors for the modest youth they had so little regarded.

"It was this famous battle which drove that warlike nation, the Crows, to go away from the Missouri and to make their home up the Yellowstone River and in the Bighorn country. But many of our men fell, and among them the brave Little Eagle!

" The sun was almost over the hills when the Sioux gathered about their campfires, recounting the honors won in battle, and naming the brave dead. Then came the singing of dirges and weeping for the slain! The sadness of loss was mingled with exultation.

" Hush! listen! the singing and wailing have ceased suddenly at both camps. There is one voice coming around the circle of campfires. It is the voice of a woman! Stripped of all her ornaments, her dress shorn of its fringes, her ankles bare, her hair cropped close to her neck, leading a pony with mane and tail cut short, she is mourning as widows mourn. It is Makátah!

" Publicly, with many tears, she declared herself the widow of the brave Little Eagle, although she had never been his wife! He it was, she said with truth, who had saved her people's honor and her life at the cost of his own. He was a true man!

" ' Ho, ho! ' was the response from many of the older warriors; but the young men, the lovers of Makátah, were surprised and sat in silence.

THE WAR MAIDEN

"The War Maiden lived to be a very old woman, but she remained true to her vow. She never accepted a husband; and all her lifetime she was known as the widow of the brave Little Eagle."

THE END

GLOSSARY

A-nó-kă-săn, white on both sides (Bald Eagle).

A-tay', father.

Chā-tŏn'-skă, White Hawk.

Chăn-ō'-tē-dah, Lives-in-the-Wood.

Chin'-tō, yes, indeed.

E-nă'-kă-nee, hurry.

E'-yă-tonk'-ă-wee, She-whose-Voice-is-heard-afar.

E-yō'-tănk-ă, rise up, or sit down.

Hă-hă'-ton-wan, Ojibway.

Hă-nă'-kă-pē, a grave.

Hăn'-tă-wō! Out of the way!

Hĕ'-chĕ-tu, it is well.

Hē-yū'-pē yā! come here!

Hī! an exclamation of thanks.

Hunk'-pă-tees, a band of Sioux.

Kă-pō-sia, Light Lodges, a band of Sioux.

Kē-chu'-wă, darling.

Kō-dă', friend.

Mă-gă'-skă-wee, Swan Maiden.

Mă-kă'-tah, Earth Woman.

Mă-tō', bear.

Mă-tō'-skă, White Bear.

Mă-tō'-să-pă, Black Bear.

Mē-chink'-shē, my son or sons.

Mē-ta', my.

GLOSSARY

Mĭn'-nē-wă-kan', Sacred Water (Devil's Lake.)

Mĭn-nē-yă'-tă, By-the-Water.

Năk-pă', Ears or Long Ears.

Nē'-nă ē-yă'-yă! run fast!

O-glu'-gē-chăn-ă, Mysterious Wood-Dweller.

Psay, snow-shoes.

Shunk'-ă, dog.

Shunk'-ă-skă, White Dog.

Shunk-ĭk'-chĕk-ă, domestic dog.

Skē-skē'-tă-tonk'-ă, Sault Sainte Marie.

Snă'-nă, Rattle.

Stă-sū', Shield (Arickaree).

Tă-ă'kē-chē-tă, his soldier.

Tă-chin'-chă-lă, fawn.

Tăk-chă, doe.

Tă-lū'-ta, Scarlet.

Tă-mă'-hay, Pike.

Tă-mă'-kō-chē, His Country.

Tă-nă'-gē-lă, Humming-Bird.

Tă-tănk'-ă-ō-tă, Many Buffaloes.

Tă-tē'-yō-pă, Her Door.

Tă-tō'-kă, Antelope.

Tă-wă-sū-ō'-tă, Many Hailstones.

Tee'-pee, tent.

Tē-yo'-tee-pee, Council lodge.

Tō'-kē-yă nun-kă' hu-wō? where are you?

Tunk-ă'-shē-dah, grandfather.

Un-chee'-dah, grandmother.

Unk'-pă-pă, a band of Sioux.

U-yă'-yō! come here!

Wă'-bă-shaw, Red Hat (name of a Sioux chief).

[278]

GLOSSARY

Wă-hă′-dah, Buyer of Furs.

Wah-pay′-ton, a band of Sioux.

Wă-hŏ′, Howler.

Wă-kăn′, sacred, mysterious.

Wăk-pay′-ku-tay, a band of Sioux.

Wă-pay′-nă, Little Barker.

Wee-kŏ′, Beautiful Woman.

Wē-nŏ′-na, Firstborn Daughter.

Wē-shă′-wee, Red Girl.

Wē′-wŏp-tay, a sharpened pole.

Wē′-yăn-nă, little woman.

Wē-zee′, Smoky Lodge.

Yănk-tŏn-nais′, a band of Sioux.

Zee-zee′-wĭn, Yellow Woman.

Zu-yă′-mă-nĭ, Walks-to-War.